PRODUCTIVITY
FOR
AUTHORS

FIND TIME TO WRITE, ORGANIZE YOUR AUTHOR
LIFE, AND DECIDE WHAT REALLY MATTERS

Joanna Penn

www.CurlUpPress.com

Contents

Introduction

"If you don't produce, you won't thrive no matter how skilled or talented you are."

Cal Newport, *Deep Work*

If you have more time to write and you use that time effectively, you will become a better writer and you will produce more books. Creativity is at the heart of what we do, but productivity is the only way to get your words out into the world.

Finished products — print books, ebooks, audiobooks — only happen when you finish your writing project. So, **you need to be productive in order to be a successful writer**.

Of course, you need to fit writing around the rest of your life, so optimizing the time you have is critical. But optimizing is not about short-term hacks. It's about sustainable productivity and doing the best you can with what you have in order to achieve more. The real question is: What do *you* want to achieve?

I've been writing and publishing for over a decade and for many of those years, I focused on 'doing.' I love making lists and ticking items off as evidence of achievement, and I am very good at getting a lot done. But a few years back, I realized that I was spending my time doing a whole load of things that weren't helping me to reach my goals. I was often busy for the sake of being busy.

I took a step back to evaluate how I was spending my time and why. I read lots of books on productivity and used many of the ideas to reboot my writing and creative business. These days, I'm much more productive in terms of what I create, but also have more time for my health and lifestyle goals. In this book, I'll share my lessons learned in order to help you become more productive and, hopefully, save you time, money and heartache along the way.

"Productivity is the amount of useful output created for every hour of work we do. Did I spend my day producing enough benefit for all the time invested?"

Seth Godin, Business/busyness

* * *

Note: There are affiliate links within this book to products and services that I recommend and use personally. This means that I receive a small percentage of sales with no extra cost to you, and in some cases, you may receive a discount for using my links. I only recommend products and services that I believe are great for authors, so I hope you find them useful.

1. What is stopping you from being productive?

Before we get started, it's important to take a step back and look at the bigger picture. No magic tool or technique is going to fix your productivity unless you also consider your mindset and the obstacles that are in your way. Be honest with yourself. There's no one here to judge you.

What is stopping you from being productive in your writing life?

Here are some common answers:

- I don't have time to write

- I don't know what to do when I have the time, so I don't spend it effectively

- I know what I have to do, and I've made the time, but I end up procrastinating and not achieving much

- I spend too much time on things like marketing, which are important and necessary for writers, but then I don't have time left over to write

Most issues relate to time and in later chapters, we'll address how to find time and make the most of your time. But at this stage, I want to challenge you to dig deeper on why you want to make a change, because you are going to have to shift your behavior if you want to achieve your goals.

What is your why?

I spent 13 years as a business IT consultant. It was great money but I didn't have anything to show for my time. Everything I did at work disappeared, because it was over-written by a new version of software or someone changed the business focus and my projects were left behind. Sure, I was paid well and I had a good lifestyle in many ways, but I was miserable and my creativity died a little more every day. In 2006, I made the decision to change my life. I was determined to leave my job and reinvent myself as an author entrepreneur.

The 'why' that drove me to the page every morning at 5 am and every evening and every weekend for years was the driving desire to leave my job, to get out of the soul-sucking, creativity-destroying situation I found myself in. Of course, I knew I had made the choices that led me there, so I made the time and did the work to get myself out of it. I finally left my consulting job in 2011 and I've never gone back.

Now **I measure my life by what I create**.

That's the 'why' that drives me these days, alongside the continued desire for freedom to spend my time on writing books, building my business instead of someone else's and helping others to pursue their creative goals through my books, podcast and website. And of course, the desire to never get another day job!

What drives you to write? Why do you want to be more productive? What is your 'why'?

Perhaps you have an inner sense that you're meant to be writing. I understand that feeling because it's common for those of us whose chosen medium of creation is the written word. Others have the same drive toward music, coding, dance, the visual arts, or other creative paths. But you need to be more specific.

Your 'why' needs to be big enough to help you through the hard times, because writing might be simple, but it's not easy. Some people talk about needing discipline to write, but for me, the word discipline has negative connotations of boot camps and drill instructors, which does not excite my creative soul!

You don't need discipline if you have a why because you have a positive reason that drives you to the page. You want to be there. So identify and write down your why and stick it somewhere you can see it.

Your self-definition can help you create

Back in 2006, I wrote down these words:

I am creative. I am an author.

I wrote them before I actually was creative or an author. It was an affirmation for my future self, but my brain had to move toward it because I repeated it every day as well as taking action, and eventually, I became those things.

When you say 'I am' about something specific, you claim the word for yourself. It focuses your mind on what you want to achieve. You obviously have to take action in a practical way, but the act of writing down an affirmation can help you to shift your self-definition which is the first step toward change.

Can you say, "I am a writer" out loud? Can you say, "I am creative. I am an author?" Or "I am a six-figure author," or whatever you want as your affirmation. Once you say even something as simple as, "I am a writer," then you must write. You must behave as a writer or you're *not* a writer.

So, who are you? What is your self-definition? When you say "I am a writer," is it reflected in how you live your life? What do writers do? Are you doing that?

> "Who you are, what you think, feel and do,
> what you love is the sum of what you focus on."
>
> Cal Newport, *Deep Work*

* * *

Questions:

- What is your why? What is driving you toward your goal? What will keep you going when things get tough?

- What is stopping you from being productive right now? What do you need to address in order to move forward?

2. Goal setting

"If you work on too many ideas at once, you run the great risk of all your ideas constantly being half finished."

Donald Roos, *Don't Read this Book:*
Time Management for Creative People

In the last chapter, you decided on your why and also considered what affirmation might help you to shift your self-definition. Now you can start to get more specific.

What is your goal?

This is the end result that you're aiming for, and if you don't have a goal in mind right now, then pick something to go through this exercise with. For example, when I was writing my first novel, I wrote down, "I will write the first draft of my novel by my birthday, March 2011." I wrote that down around 15 months before the date.

Writing is project-based work, so there will be goals at different times of the creative cycle: Planning, idea generation and research; writing a first draft; editing; publishing and marketing, before cycling back to the beginning again. As your writing career matures, you might have different books in different stages of the process at the same time, but regardless of where you are, you need to decide on your goal.

Writing down a specific endpoint gives you direction and keeps you accountable

A goal has an end date and is measurable, so you will know whether or not you have achieved it. Writers write, so write your goal down and stick it somewhere you can see it.

Of course, you may change your goals over time, but they set you off in a specific direction — and we all have to choose a direction or we end up going in circles.

Pick one primary goal to focus on

Beware of choosing too many major goals at the same time, something many people do at the New Year. For example, you decide to write a book and run a marathon in the next six months. Those are two big goals that both take time and great effort. Imagine yourself at a crossroads with a big wooden sign with two directions indicated: Train for marathon and Write a book. Each will take hours of your time every week and it's unlikely you can achieve both at the same time. Decide which one of those you want to achieve now and do the other one later.

You can achieve a lot in your life, but you can't do it all at once, so move in the direction of your primary goal.

Choose different goals for different stages

There are stages to the author journey. You will have different goals over time and you will also require different types of productivity.

If you're a brand-new writer and you've never written a book before, you need to focus on writing your first draft. You need more words on the page, more time to think and create, so set aside time for publishing and marketing later. Don't try to learn everything at once.

If you're an established author with a number of books, you understand the process of writing, publishing and marketing, so productivity is more about task juggling. How do you write more in the time you have? How can you increase your income? How do you run a more effective creative business?

* * *

Questions:

- What goals do you currently have in your life? What is your primary goal?

- What stage of the author journey are you at? What is the best goal for your current stage? What could wait until later?

3. Deadlines

Once you have a goal, you need to set a deadline.

Some people don't like deadlines, but personally, I think they're critical for getting things done, especially when there is no external pressure to finish a project. If you're writing the first draft of your first book, there is no one to say you must complete it by a certain date. If you're an indie author with no traditional publishing contract, then no one is pushing you to achieve a publication date. You have to drive yourself, and deadlines help you to do this.

Writing is a creative process and as such, is considered by some to be 'above' the structured imposition of a deadline, but if you want to take your writing from the page to the finished form of a book, you need to set deadlines.

If you're still resisting this idea, consider it from the creative perspective. Creativity is like a vertical pipe — you put things in the top, things you read and watch and experience, and then they get all mushed up together and emerge out the bottom as an idea or as written words. You need to keep the flow going by continuing to consume, but also by continuing to produce, or it will block up.

In my experience, the more you produce, the more creativity comes down the pipe. That's when things get exciting. Of course, I still remember when I didn't have any ideas, when I believed I wasn't creative, so don't worry if you're there right now. But trust me, once you get into it, once you get that pipe moving, ideas will not be the problem. The problem will be finding enough time to write everything you want to write in your lifetime.

Accountability will help you to achieve your writing goal

If you surround yourself with people aiming for the same goal, it can encourage you to achieve yours.

Back in 2006, when I started writing, I didn't know any writers, but over time, I met people on Twitter and then at live events. I went to meetups and conferences and had coffee dates with other authors and now I'm part of a thriving community. But like everything, it takes time and effort on your part.

Look for a writing group near you or a Facebook group, or you can use Twitter to find other writers. Check out #5amwritersclub and #writingcommunity. There are lots of places to find writers at all stages of the journey.

If you want to write a novel, you could join NaNoWriMo. org, which is how I started writing my first novel in 2009. You can find Writing Sprint groups online or do a writing course in person. After NaNoWriMo, I joined Year of the Novel at the Queensland Writers' Centre in Brisbane, Australia. I attended classes at weekends but the course structure also gave me deadlines to produce chapters, which helped me to finish my first novel, which eventually became *Stone of Fire*.

> I documented my journey from first ideas to published novel at:
>
> TheCreativePenn.com/firstnovel

You could also use a blog or podcast to document your journey. A lot of my success comes from the fact I have been writing and podcasting on TheCreativePenn.com since December 2008. When I started, I had one non-fiction book, and everything has grown since then.

I write because I measure my life by what I create, but I also have a reputation and a responsibility to my community. If I'm not writing, how can I blog or podcast about writing? How can I help others on the author entrepreneur journey if I'm not moving forward myself? That keeps me going when things are difficult, and it's great to have the accountability of my audience.

Of course, when I started out, I didn't have an audience and we all start with nothing, but by putting your goal and your thoughts out there on the Internet, you will feel more accountable and attract an audience and community. However, this does take time that you could use for writing, so you need to decide what works for you.

Work out how much time you need for your book

Once you've written a few books, you will understand your process and approximately how long you need to write a first draft. But if you're just starting out, you'll need to set a deadline that takes into account the time you need.

You can do this by working out approximately how many words your book will be, based on your genre, and how many words you write per hour.

In traditional publishing, fantasy novels are 100,000 - 120,000 words, while romance is often shorter, at 50,000 to 70,000. Thrillers are 70,000 - 90,000. Non-fiction books and memoir are usually 50,000 to 70,000 words. If you're writing children's books, shorter novellas or non-fiction, they might be around 30,000 words.

If you're unsure, find a book that's similar to the one you're aiming to write and figure out the word count. Multiply the page count by the number of words per page. Count along the top of the page and then count the lines. This is just a rough approximation, but it helps to start somewhere.

Let's take 70,000 words as an example.

> If you can write 1,000 words an hour, it's going to take you 70 hours to write a first draft.

Of course, you need thinking and planning time before you write, and more time to edit later, but without a first draft, you will never get to editing. So, make your first goal finishing that first draft, and you can add time blocks for editing later.

If you can carve out five hours a week for writing, that's 5,000 words per week, so it will take you **14 weeks to write 70,000 words of a first draft.**

Add some extra time for thinking, plotting and a buffer, and you're at 16 weeks, or four months to produce a first draft. You can do the same calculation for pages edited per day. Set your first deadline four months away. Get out your calendar, count the months and put in your deadline date. Write it down next to your goal where you can see it.

* * *

Questions:

- What is the deadline for your goal? Have you written it down somewhere you can see it regularly?

- What can you do to make yourself more accountable?

4. Busy work vs. important work

"The biggest waste of time is to do well something that we need not do at all."

Gretchen Rubin, *Better Than Before*

If you feel like you have too much to do, that you're overwhelmed with tasks in all areas of your life, then this section is for you.

You're probably eager to get to the chapters on finding time to write and making the most of that time. Don't worry, they're coming soon! But this chapter is important to go through first, because a lot of productivity problems stem from doing too many of the wrong things.

Productivity means spending time on the things you *want* to achieve instead of ticking off a list of things you didn't want to do in the first place. Perhaps you didn't know you didn't want to do them until you were in the middle of the process, but now's the time to stop doing, take a breath and think.

I know that's hard. I'm a 'doer.' I like ticking things off my To Do list every day. I'm a Type A personality, goal-focused, and I achieve a lot. But my biggest mistakes have come from moving fast to achieve something I didn't think about in the first place and later didn't even want.

The trick to being more productive is to eliminate tasks, not add more of them

The first step to elimination is acknowledging what you have on your plate. So write everything down, get it out of your head and onto a piece of paper, or into an app, or whatever you prefer to use.

Include everything that's not writing-related as well. Maybe you've started a home improvement project or there's a big birthday coming up that you need to organize. Maybe your child has a soccer tournament or you need to exercise more. Maybe you're trying to make a list of agents to pitch and then there's that online course you need to finish … and it goes on! Whatever is going on for you, write it down. Big stuff, small stuff. It's all taking up space in your head, so write it down.

Once you've written it all down, have a look at the list.

How much is busy work? How much can wait until a later stage in the process?

For example, many writers want to know the details of the publishing process before they have even written a first draft, but most people who start a book never finish it. Don't clutter your mind with things you don't need to focus on right now.

If you're further along on your author journey, your list most likely includes lots of things you should be doing around book marketing. But how many of those are necessary right now and how many can wait?

I know this is hard because I *like* being busy. It makes me feel like I've achieved something. But over and over again, I have found myself busy with things that don't really matter. Time passes and opportunities are lost.

You can't do everything. If you try to work on a lot of projects at the same time, you won't achieve your goals. But if you stop and work on one of them, take it all the way to completion and then start on the next one, you're going to be more productive.

If you don't want to cross things off your list, then move items that can wait somewhere else. The list will still be there, but when you revisit those things later, they might not seem so important.

Balancing busy work, important work and urgent work

If your goal is to be a writer, writing and working on your author career is important work that is not urgent and does not necessarily give you an immediate return on your time. It may not feel like you have achieved something and ticked something off your list after each writing session, but if you don't do it, you will never reach your goal.

> A lot of the time, we don't do our important work because of urgent or busy work.

Maybe your child is sick and you need to take them to the doctor urgently. Or water starts coming through the kitchen ceiling. You drop everything to do what needs to be done. But these things are not everyday occurrences so you just need to accept that they happen sometimes. Urgent work is rarely the problem: busy work is.

Housework is busy work. Social media is definitely busy work! You accomplish something, it takes up time, and you get the satisfaction of achieving a very short-term task, but does it really move you toward your goal? Responding to email is necessary busy work, but do you need to respond immediately? Can you batch busy work and do it in a scheduled time slot later?

Categorize your list in terms of these different buckets: busy, important or urgent. How much of that busy work do you *really* have to do? What can you move to the Later list? Could you eliminate or outsource? We'll go into this in more detail in Chapter 10 on outsourcing.

"Busy is not your job. Busy doesn't get you what you seek. Busy isn't the point. Value creation is."

Seth Godin

* * *

Questions:

- Write down everything you have to do, or review your list. How much of it is 'busy work'? How much can wait until a later stage of the process?

- How are you balancing busy work with important work and urgent work? What things fall into these categories for you?

5. Saying no and setting boundaries

Hopefully you've culled your bulging To Do list after the previous chapter, but I'll bet it still has a lot on it. If you don't take control, it will end up growing again by the end of the week.

Create your Not To Do list

This is where you need to make some choices, because you can't do everything all at once. It's just not possible.

I used to do a lot of professional speaking, but even though it brought in money and helped people, it took a lot of time to prepare, do the event and then recover afterwards. As part of rebooting my productivity, I decided that 2019 would be my 'year of no speaking' and I said to no to everyone who asked. It made such a difference to make that decision in advance and I didn't feel guilty about saying no. I didn't feel like I was missing out. My 'Not To Do' list had public speaking on it, so I didn't speak, and it freed up so much time and head space. I reach people with my voice through my podcast so I can help those who need it without being physically present.

I have lots of other things on my Not To Do list, but my life is not the same as yours, so the details are not important. The real question is, what needs to go on *your* Not To Do list?

You have to make choices based on your goal and your deadline and you might have to say no to a good opportunity, something you actually want to do. But can it wait until a later date?

Chances are, if you're not feeling productive enough, then **you need to set some boundaries — not just with other people, but also with yourself.**

Sometimes, you will have to fight against social expectation and things you feel you want to be doing for other reasons. For example, you realize that you can make an extra three hours per week for your writing if you give up supervising after-school activities or volunteering at church. But these are good things for you and your community, so where will you set your boundaries?

Set your boundaries for a limited time

This is how I managed to stop speaking for a year, carving out a LOT of extra time for creation and learning new skills like audiobook narration. I decided that 2019 would be the year of no speaking, but I would speak again in 2020, and repeat that pattern going forward so I can maintain balance.

You could do the same. For example, tell the school or the church that you need three months or six months off and then return later on. Switch things up to carve out time and make it up later if you feel guilty.

"Guard your time well, do fewer things well."

Donald Roos, *Don't Read this Book:*
Time Management for Creative People

Batch your work

If you really do need to keep a lot of those things on your list, then batch your work. For example, schedule all meetings on certain days of the week, so you have bigger blocks available for creation. Or do a batch of cooking at the weekend so you can carve out some extra writing time in the evenings. Task switching is often a problem for productivity, but if you batch tasks, you can get a lot done at once, leaving more time for your writing.

Embrace the joy of missing out

Social media is generally responsible for the fear of missing out. It makes us feel like we must be at every event and be part of every conversation.

But you need to embrace missing out if you want to claim back your time. You need to think, "I'm enjoying being at home writing my book instead of going to that conference because it will help me reach my goals more quickly." Your examples will differ, but you have to establish boundaries for yourself as well as others.

Are you in control of your time or do other people control your priorities?

Obviously, if you have kids and a day job, a lot of your time is controlled by other people, but there are ways you can control distractions and interruptions.

Do you have notifications on your phone that make noises all the time? Do you leave your phone on when you're doing other things? If the phone rings, do you always answer it? Do you open email several times an hour and lose track of what else you were doing? Do you schedule creation time somewhere where the kids can't interrupt you?

If you get rid of distractions — your phone, social media, email — at least for chunks of time, you will be more creative. You'll be able to write more.

Still struggling?

If you're struggling, check out Freedom.to, an app that blocks the Internet for a certain time period. This takes the choice away from you. You could set it up so that between 5:00 and 5:45 a.m., it blocks everything. You have to turn your phone off and on again to override the settings.

Another common distraction is too much news media, especially in the political environment we now live in. But the world will carry on while you're writing and you can check your news apps once you're finished. I'm definitely a news junkie, but I control my addiction by only reading the news with paid subscriptions to respected media so it is curated and not sensationalized. I know what's going on. I just don't want the distraction of over-the-top media on TV.

There are many other distractions. It might be gaming, or arguing on Twitter, or scrolling through Instagram, or watching 'really useful' YouTube videos. We all have things that distract us, but we need to get rid of those in order to create.

The list will never stop. There will always be more demands on your time. 'Later' will never come unless you make the time now.

"The single most important change you can make in your working habits is to switch to creative work first, reactive work second."

Jocelyn K. Glei, *Manage Your-Day-To-Day*

* * *

Questions:

- What are you struggling to say no to? Where do you need to set boundaries to protect your creative time?

- Write your own Not To Do list

- How much are you giving into distraction? Have you turned off notifications on your phone and computer?

- What could you do if you are still struggling?

6. How to find the time to write

Finding time to write is the most important step in writing more, but how do you find the time? In the previous chapters, we started on the process of culling your To Do list, and now we're going to take it a step further. Because after over a decade of writing and more than 30 books published, I've found there is only one answer.

Schedule your writing time

Seriously, this could be a transformational step if you've not done this before. It's not complicated. Get out your calendar or your smartphone app or however you schedule your time, and put in slots for writing.

Then show up for that time to write just as you would show up for a business meeting or a gym class or anything else that is time-sensitive. Stop making your writing slot optional or showing up late as if it doesn't matter.

As Stephen King says in *On Writing*, **"Don't wait for the muse.** Your job is to make sure the muse knows where you're going to be every day, from 9:00 till noon, or 7:00 till 3:00. If he does know, I assure you that sooner or later he'll start showing up."

You can understand the muse as a metaphor or as more literal if you prefer. Steven Pressfield, author of *The War of Art*, invokes the muse before he writes in the classical sense of asking the divine to help inspire his work. Whatever works for you.

I know that if I show up to the page, eventually something's going to happen. When I'm working on a first draft, I sit down for my scheduled writing session from 7:00 am until around 9:30-10 am. I take a break, then maybe do another session later on in the day.

If I'm sitting at my specific table in my local café, my creative brain knows I'm there to write or edit. I don't have any other tasks booked in for that time. If I turn up for my scheduled writing slot, I'm far more likely to write something than if I wait until I have a spare moment. Because let's face it, no one ever has a spare moment!

If you don't already use a planning calendar, then it's time to start

You must, must, must schedule your writing time. Presumably, you schedule other things in your life, like going to the day job or your kid's school events, or your dentist appointment, or going to the gym regularly, or whatever. That's how you need to schedule your writing.

But what if you try to schedule your writing time and can't find a slot?

Track how you spend your time now

This can be challenging and can also be a shock. I did this back when I wanted to write my first non-fiction book in 2006-2007. I looked at my time and realized that I went to the gym in the morning, then I went to work, then I would come home exhausted, make dinner, and sometimes we'd watch three hours of TV before bed. That was every night, or at least most nights in a week.

When I discovered the amount of time I was watching TV, consuming rather than producing, I decided to cut back. TV is a lot better these days, but if you're watching three hours a night, you can definitely cut back, too. I also know authors who gave up gaming when they became writers, or at least rationed their gaming hours, as it can be such a time suck.

What about the gym and exercise time? We all need to stay healthy, and I'll come back to health in Chapter 13, but maybe there are things you can change. For example, in the last couple of years, I've been walking ultra-marathons, so in training for that, I would spend eight to ten hours walking. In that time, I listened to a lot of audiobooks and sometimes did a bit of dictation. When I realized I needed that time back, I switched to spin class and yoga, which take up less time, and I can still achieve my health goals with a longer walk on Sundays.

If you're going to prioritize your writing, you have to change something. I don't recommend you cut out sleep, but there are ways you can optimize it, for example, go to bed earlier, get up earlier and write in the early morning.

If you're still struggling to find the time, here's some tough love.

How much do you really want this?

What is your why and what are you willing to give up for your goal? Because something has to give.

There are a few other things I did to make time between 2006 and 2011 when I had a day job, before I went full-time as an author entrepreneur. I wrote my first four books in those years, blogged at The Creative Penn, started pod-casting and learned about all the things that are needed to build and grow a creative business.

I worked a demanding day job but I still made time to write.

I got up at 5 a.m. to write before work. I was never going to be able to write after work because I was exhausted by the time I came home. That morning session was always for writing or editing or working on a book, and the extra time I had in the evenings after cutting down TV was for marketing and building my author platform.

I opted out of the career ladder. If you have a day job and you're doing everything you can to advance up that career ladder, you will often do a lot more than your official job requires. You'll put in more hours and often work from home, taking up more time but also headspace that you can't use for your writing.

So, I mentally opted out of my consulting career. I knew I didn't want to follow that path and I didn't want to become a manager. I wanted to do my work, then leave on time. I also worked from home as much as possible, often with two laptops open so I could fit in creative business tasks alongside my day job work.

I eventually **moved to working four days a week at the day job**, essentially cutting 20% of my income and 20% of the time that I had to spend at work. Of course, you often have to get as much done in four days as they ask you to do in five, but it helps if you don't have to commute, check email and answer phone calls on that other day. You can just focus on writing.

That was how I made the time, but of course, you will have to find what works for you.

Where can you carve out time?

"Write at the edges of the day."

Toni Morrison

It doesn't need to be big chunks. You don't need a two-hour block to get more writing done. I know of one particular author with five children who keeps her laptop in the kitchen and somehow writes while managing her hectic family life. She has around 50 novels written over the years of child-rearing.

For other people, it's **writing when the children are asleep** in the early morning or late evening. I mentioned TV and gaming, and the other thing that takes time is household tasks. I've outsourced my cleaning for the last decade, which has freed up a lot more of my time.

How about combining activities? For example, write while commuting. Mark Dawson, bestselling thriller author, wrote his first five novels while commuting by train for a few hours each day. If you walk or you're in the car, you could try dictating, covered in Chapter 8.

Once you have time blocks available in your calendar, schedule in the number you need in order to get to your goal. You calculated this in Chapter 3 on deadlines. Using that example, if you carve out five hours a week for writing, that's 5,000 words per week, so it will take you **14 weeks to write 70,000 words of a first draft.**

Get out your schedule and put in your weekly blocks for 14 weeks. That might be one hour per week day or maybe three blocks in the week and a two-hour session at the weekend. Whatever works for you: But you do need to actually schedule it. Don't skip this step.

When you see the time block in your calendar, it is not optional. If you're tempted to skip it, say to yourself, "My writing is important. I will be there at that time and I will write."

If you do that, you will achieve your goal. Find the time, turn up, do the work and then carry on with your busy life.

No one said this was going to be easy

If it was easy, everyone would be writing a book. Everyone *says* they're writing a book, but in order to actually achieve your goal, you have to turn up and do the work.

Some surveys say that 80% of people *want* to write a book, but very few of those people end up publishing, and even fewer of those end up making a good living with their writing. So the question is, **who do you want to be?**

> "On the field of the Self, stand a knight and a dragon.
> You are the knight, resistance is the dragon.
> The battle must be fought every day."

> Steven Pressfield, *The War of Art*

I've had this quote on my wall for years. I wrote it out in ink a long time ago and it's faded now but I know it off by heart because the battle must indeed be fought every day. Even if you schedule those 14 weeks of time blocks into your calendar, what happens at 6 a.m. on a cold morning as you lie in bed and think, "I really don't want to do this. What's the point? I'll just have another hour in bed." There will always be things that will get in your way, and your mind may be your greatest challenge.

You must fight that resistance if you want to succeed as a writer. Get up and do your work.

* * *

Questions:

- Are you scheduling your writing time at the moment? If not, why not? Where is your resistance?

- Do you have an accurate view of how you spend your time? If not, track a week of activities including TV and gaming.

- What are you going to give up in order to find time for your writing?

- Have you done the calculation on how much time you need for that first draft? Or revision time or whatever you need.

- Have you scheduled your next block of writing time?

7. Make the most of your writing time

Now you've carved out the time and scheduled the writing sessions that will help you to achieve your goal, what can you do to make the most effective use of your writing time?

(1) Choose the right location

There are no rules, but I suggest that your writing place should be different to the places you do other things.

Humans are habitual creatures. We like doing the same things in the same place and it sets off a certain frame of mind. I have a home office where I do my podcasting, interviews, email, accounting and other business tasks. I cannot write or edit my books at the same desk.

I write my first drafts and edit at a local café. I go early when it opens so they have tables spare and I buy a black coffee every hour in exchange for the writing space. Most people come for takeaways at that time of day and I'm gone before the rush after 10 am. If you like to work in a cafe, make sure to respect the business and be a good customer so they're happy to have you there.

When I'm working on my laptop, I use a Nexstand riser and external keyboard for ergonomic positioning. If I'm editing, I print out the whole manuscript and edit by hand. I sometimes edit at home on the dining room table, but never in my office.

It helps to keep my spaces separate, because when I'm in my home office, there is always more to do on the business, but when I'm at the café, I'm only there for one reason. To create something new in the world.

You could go to the library or hire a desk or a room in a co-working space, common in most cities now. If I'm working to a first draft deadline, I will often hire a local room for dictation in addition to my morning café sessions. It costs me around US$15 per hour. If I cancel too late, then I'll have to pay for it anyway, so it forces me to turn up. This accountability helps, especially if I don't feel like writing, and it enables me to finish the first draft more quickly.

Of course, the writing process is not just about getting words on a page. This creative time slot is for whatever phase of the creative project that you're in. It might be planning or plotting, research, outlining, first draft writing or editing. But don't mix it up with publishing or marketing activities which use other parts of your brain. Keep one special location for your creative tasks.

(2) Get into the right mindset — quickly

"The last thing I do before I sit down to work is say my prayer to the Muse. I say it out loud, in absolute earnest. Only then do I get down to business."

Steven Pressfield, *The War of Art*

Many writers use a ritual to get into the creative mindset but it is specific to them and not some magic way that can be used by others.

So, don't get obsessed with finding a perfect ritual, but do establish a routine and a habit around your writing practice, so you can switch into your writing mindset quickly and get on with your work.

I go to the café and sit at a specific table, order my black coffee, put on my noise-canceling headphones with Rain and Thunderstorms on repeat, then write.

I use Bose QuietComfort noise-canceling headphones and I love them. I also wear them on airplanes and anywhere noise gets to me. As an introvert, I'm highly sensitive to sound. They're pricey but they're seriously one of the best investments I've ever made in my writing, creativity and productivity.

I've also been listening to the same Rain and Thunderstorms album for over a decade. What a bargain! You can also use the RainyMood app or find free ambient sounds online to shut out other noise. As soon as the rain starts, my brain knows I'm in a creative space. Nothing else matters. I almost don't hear it anymore, but you will find a storm in almost all of my novels, so it must have some influence!

If you like more exciting music or you're interested in what other writers listen to, check out the Undercover Soundtrack blog by Roz Morris which features authors and the soundtracks for their books. I'm definitely the most boring person ever in terms of my listening habits while I write, but it works for me. You need to find what works for you.

(3) Turn off distractions

Turn off your phone and any notifications. Put it on airplane mode or silent. If you're worried about an emergency with your kids or your job, put your phone on vibrate but do whatever you can to stop yourself looking at it during the writing session.

No multitasking. In this specific block of writing time, you are not allowed to do anything else other than work on your book. If you're writing a first draft, then write the first draft. If you're editing, then edit. If you know that you will end up going down an Internet rabbit-hole of research, then turn off the Internet. Just put a note in the document and come back to it later.

Stop making excuses. Do the work.

(4) Use timed writing

Timed writing changed my life back in the days when I still dreamed of being a writer. One year, I went to a creative writing class at the Sydney Writers' Festival. I'm a very good student, so I had my notebook at the ready to write down pearls of wisdom. I was prepared to listen and learn. But then the teacher said, "The first thing we're going do is write for ten minutes about a day when you discovered something that would change your life." He looked at his watch. "Ten minutes. Off you go."

Everyone around me started writing fast as I sat there for a moment, stunned. You mean I actually have to write something? As I picked up my pen, I realized that I had not faced a timed writing exercise since school exams, and it was definitely my first time with a creative writing prompt.

But I started writing anyway, and after ten minutes, I had a couple of paragraphs about a particular memory. It shocked me and changed my life, because I really didn't think I could create from my brain like that. It pushed me past my self-doubt and I started using timed writing sessions for everything.

In 2009, I did NaNoWriMo, National Novel Writing Month, and I used timed writing to get my first 20,000 words down. I eventually turned those words into the beginning of *Stone of Fire*.

You can try writing sprints if you're in a writing group online or off. You could also try NaNoWriMo.org in November when lots of people write at the same time. You'll often find writing groups in your town during this period.

There are also habit-tracking apps that you can use with writing timers, or check out the Pomodoro Technique, developed by Francesco Cirillo. You can find information about that online.

You may find other techniques useful, but timed writing was the thing that got me over myself. Don't just sit down and see what you can come up with in an hour. Do several timed blocks with a little break in between and you will achieve more in the same time.

(5) Stop procrastinating

If you're still struggling with checking email and social media, or gaming apps, whatever else you're procrastinating with, you need to **be self-aware** enough to say, "I've got to stop this."

Put your phone on airplane mode and turn off notifications. How many times do I have to say this?! Seriously, I've been to so many writing events where authors will have notifications coming through constantly. *Ping, ping, ping.* Don't do that!

If you're still struggling, **schedule a procrastination break.** Say to yourself, "I know my brain needs to procrastinate, so, I'm going to write for 20 minutes and then I'm going to stop and have a social media or email break," or whatever you need. Set a timer for five minutes so you don't lose track of time, then get back to writing.

"The professional shows up every day.
The professional is committed over the long haul.
The amateur tweets, the pro works."

Steven Pressfield, *Turning Pro*

I reread *Turning Pro* every new year because it continues to challenge me in my creative life because I do tweet @ TheCreativePenn. I like tweeting and it serves my business. I like Instagram, too. Social media has its place, but not when it takes your writing time.

(6) Measure your progress

It can be really hard to see your progress, especially in the first draft of your first book. In your mind, you can see a finished book. It's amazing! But then you sit down and write 500 words and realize you have a long way to go. And you do. But everything worth doing takes time!

There are a number of ways you can measure your progress. I use **Project Targets** on Scrivener, which has a progress bar that turns from red to green for each writing session and also for the book as a whole. Many writers use **spreadsheets or apps** to track word count.

I used a **physical wall calendar** when I started out, as it keeps creation top of mind. I used colored pens and stickers to reward my creative self. Who doesn't love a sticker for good work?

I'd get a sticker for 2,000+ words in a session, and if I was under, I'd just write the word count in a colored pen. One month, I logged 42,905 words that way and it was motivating to see the word count add up over the days. This idea of 'don't break the chain,' or 'don't break the streak,' is common in habit formation, and it's a great idea if you're in first draft mode. Word count matters less when you're in editing or other stages of the creative process, but you might still log hours spent on the project or pages edited.

In James Clear's book, *Atomic Habits*, he suggests filling a jar with paperclips and putting an empty jar beside it. Each paperclip could represent a writing session, or a thousand words, or whatever is appropriate. After each session, move a paper clip from one jar to the other and over time, the originally empty jar will fill up and you can see your progress. You might feel like you haven't achieved much in one writing session, but if you focus on the process rather than the finished product, you will see progress over time.

"Habit tracking keeps your eye on the ball. You're focused on the process rather than the results. It's remarkable what you can build if you just don't stop."

James Clear, *Atomic Habits*

(7) Know what you're going to write before you write it

This is definitely a way to make the most of your writing time, but how you do this will depend on the kind of writer you are. I'm a discovery writer, so I don't outline. However, on my walk to the cafe or the days between, or out on a walk, I'll be thinking about my characters or the topic I want to write about for non-fiction, and I might jot down some notes, or think about possibilities, so that when I sit down to write, I know what I'm there to do or at least have a starting point.

Other writers swear by an outline, perhaps a few lines or paragraph per chapter which you can expand during your writing time. Some authors, like thriller author Jeffrey

Deaver, write extensive outlines. Of course, you don't have to do it all in advance. You could spend five to ten minutes at the beginning of your writing session thinking about what you will write. Jot down a few bullet points and then expand them in your writing session.

(8) Spend more hours in the chair

Authors who are massively productive spend more of their time writing. Fantasy author Lindsay Buroker will sometimes write for eight hours a day. She can write a book a month because she puts in the hours. I have *never* written for eight hours in a single day so it takes me longer to put the hours in so I don't produce as many books.

If you spend more hours in the writing chair, you are going to spend more time writing. You will write more words per day as a result.

If you don't have more hours in the day, then carve out **more writing sessions in the week**. If you're managing one hour, three times a week, but you want to be more productive with your writing, then do one hour, six times a week. You will double the number of words written and get to your goal faster.

(9) No excuses

What if you don't feel like writing? What if you're too tired or you've got a headache?

Would you go to your day job in your current condition? Are you taking your writing just as seriously?

Obviously, if you're really sick, then no worries. Take a break. But many people go to their day job when they don't 'feel' like it, or they're tired, or they have a headache. They still manage to get their work done even if they're not in the mood.

There are days when I sit down to write and I find it so hard. I really don't want to be there. Then another day it feels amazing. I'm in flow and everything is brilliant. But the truth is, you will not be able to tell the difference between those two pieces of writing when you read the book later. It makes no difference to the finished product.

No excuses. Do your work.

"Don't wait for the muse … he's a hardheaded guy who's not susceptible to a lot of creative fluttering. This isn't the Ouija board or the spirit-world we're talking about here, but just another job like laying pipe or driving long-haul trucks."

Stephen King, *On Writing*

* * *

Questions:

- What does your creative setup and ritual look like?

- How will you stop distractions and interruptions?

- Have you tried timed writing? If not, why not?

- How will you measure your progress?

- How could you write faster?

- Are there any other ways that will help you make the most of your time writing?

8. Dictation

When most people say they are writing a book, they tend to mean typing with their fingers on a computer keyboard. Before typewriters, people only thought about writing by hand, with a pen or a quill. Before that, it might have been carving symbols onto stone.

But think about the end result.

A book is a **mode of communication between your brain and the brain of a reader.** How it gets there is not so important. Creating by voice (dictation) and consuming by listening to voice (audiobooks and podcasts) are becoming more common in an age of increasing digital speed — and dictation can be a superpower when it comes to productivity.

A number of famous authors wrote, or still write, with dictation. John Milton of Paradise Lost, Dan Brown, Henry James, Barbara Cartland, the incredibly prolific romance author, and Winston Churchill. You probably couldn't get two more different people than Barbara Cartland and Winston Churchill!

When Terry Pratchett, author of the *Discworld* fantasy series, couldn't write anymore because of early-onset Alzheimer's, he moved into dictation. I've written parts of a number of my books with dictation and in fact, the first draft of this book was dictated and transcribed. Clearly, it's an effective mode of creation.

Why consider dictation for your writing?

Writing speed and stamina improves with dictation. It's much faster to speak words than it is to type them, especially if you can get out of your own way and stop self-censoring. I can type around 2,000-3,000 words in a first draft writing session of two hours, but with dictation, I can get up to 5,000 words in the same period.

There is definitely a trade-off. Until you improve at dictation, your words won't be as polished as typing them at a slower pace. You'll need to do an editing pass. But sometimes just getting the rough draft down as fast as possible is useful and then you can go back and edit. The trade-off reduces over time as you get better at dictation.

Another benefit is **increased creativity**. Many writers suffer from perfectionism when typing. They obsessively correct and retype the same paragraphs over and over again because a first draft for a beginning writer is not going to be fantastic. If you keep rewriting in this early stage, you may never finish the book, but dictating bypasses that critical voice because no one expects speech to be perfect and you know you can fix it later.

Dictation is healthier. Many people get into dictation because they suffer from Repetitive Strain Injury or some kind of pain that impacts their ability to type. Or they realize they need to make a change to the writer's sedentary life and move more. Even if you don't need dictation now, you may need it later, especially if you want to make a living with your writing for the long term. Consider dictation as a way to future-proof your career as a writer. Hopefully, you can avoid health issues, but if you do ever suffer from them, you have other ways of creating.

If dictation is so amazing, why isn't everyone doing it?

Here are some of the most common issues, and I know these very well, because I have said all of these things myself!

- I'm used to typing. I don't have the right kind of brain for dictation.

- I don't want to say the punctuation out loud. It will disrupt my flow.

- I write in public so I can't dictate.

- I have a difficult accent which will make it impossible for the speech to text software.

- I write fantasy books with weird names that I can't possibly dictate.

- I don't know how to set it up technically.

- I can't spare the time to learn how to dictate.

- I can't afford the software.

These are all valid concerns, but this is a book on productivity, so if dictation can make your writing process more effective, it's worth considering.

I've found that dictation really helps to get that first draft down so I can move into editing. I don't use it on every book but when I have, it's made the process faster, but I still resisted it!

Here's my journal entry on the first day I tried dictation.

"I'm very self-conscious. I'm worried that I won't be able to find the words. I'm so used to typing and creating through my fingers that doing it with my voice feels strange.

But **I learned to type with my fingers, so why can't I learn to type with my words?** I just have to practice. Something will shift in my mind at some point and it will just work.

This should make me a healthier author and also someone who writes faster. Authors who use dictation are writing incredibly fast. That's what I want. I want to write stories faster, as I have so many in my mind that I want to get into the world."

Here's my journal entry *after* the first session:

"It felt like the words were really bad and the story clunky and poor, but actually when the transcription was done and I lightly edited it, **it wasn't as bad as I thought it would be**. A classic case of critical voice. I need to ignore this when I'm dictating.

I definitely need to plan more before I speak, which will save time overall in both dictation and editing. I thought I would find the punctuation difficult, but it has also been easier than expected. There are only a few commands that you use regularly, and dialogue is the worst, but you get into a rhythm with that. It also gives you a pause between each speaker to consider what they might say next. So perhaps it is a blessing in disguise."

I hope these journal entries help you in terms of addressing fear before you start. Once you get into it, you realize that it's not that bad after all. You just have to try it yourself.

There are different methods of dictation.

(1) Speech to text in real time

There are lots of programs for speech to text now and most computers have a speech to text or dictation mode for word processing programs.

Nuance Dragon is the most well-known software and they have an app, Dragon Anywhere, for mobile use but it can be pricey. Try these other options for starters:

- Open Google Docs on Chrome Browser. Click Tools -> Voice Typing

- On the Mac, use Edit -> Start Dictation

- On the PC, hold down the Windows key and press H to trigger the dictation toolbar. (This may vary with whatever version of Windows you're on.)

Once dictation is enabled, speak directly into the computer and words will appear on the screen. Accuracy will improve with a separate microphone, but you can start with just your usual computer setup. Edit as you dictate or fix it up later.

You can use voice commands to do a whole lot more and if you do have health issues and you can't use your arms or hands much, then that's probably the mode you want to use. Personally, I don't like to look at the screen as I dictate, as it engages my critical voice.

(2) Dictate now, transcribe later

This is my preferred method of dictation and how I wrote the first draft of this book. I record the chapters and then get it transcribed. Again, there are a lot of options for this and the price for transcription is coming down fast because of artificial intelligence so look around for the latest options.

Here are a few:

- If you have Dragon, upload the MP3 in Transcription mode to produce a .txt file

- If you prefer a human, use Speechpad.com or Rev.com

- AI transcription is cheaper and improving all the time, so check out services like Trint.com or Otter.ai as well as Descript.com which also offers audio editing.

Once you get your transcription back, just a few minutes later if you're using software or AI services, you can do a first pass edit to fix up any punctuation or typos. I copy and paste my transcribed files into Scrivener, lightly edit it with one pass and then properly edit after the first draft is complete.

Technical setup

As above, you don't have to spend any money. You can use free apps on your phone to record and free software like Google Docs for dictation, so don't let fear of technical setup get in the way of trying it. But of course, if you do want to improve accuracy, there are a few things you can do.

The quality of your microphone makes a difference, as does making sure to record in a quiet environment. If the software can understand your voice more easily, the transcription will obviously be better.

For first draft recording, I use a handheld Sony ICD-PX333 MP3 recorder which you can find at: TheCreativePenn.com/sony

I just hold it near my mouth and use the Pause button in between thoughts. You can also use a Lavalier (or lav) lapel microphone that plugs into your phone if you want to walk and talk.

> When recording directly into the computer, I use a Blue Yeti microphone, which I also use for my podcast and recording my online courses:

> TheCreativePenn.com/blueyeti

I used to use Speechpad.com for transcription but as AI transcription improved, I started using Trint and then Descript as the latter also allow audio editing which I use for my podcast and audiobooks. However, software changes fast and prices continue to drop, so I'd recommend you search online for the best services.

Tips from writers who dictate

Kevin J. Anderson is an incredibly productive author with hundreds of books published, most of which he dictated while hiking.

> "The biggest advice that I would give for you and other writers to get started with dictation is don't try to write that way. **The best way is to start to do notes or brainstorming.** Take your recorder and go for a walk. It's almost like free association.

> When you're starting out, don't think that you have to do full sentences. Maybe **use your first round of dictation to plot and plan and get notes down.** That can be a really good way to get started with dictation."

Kevin has a book on dictation, *On Being a Dictator: Using Dictation to be a Better Writer.*

Monica Leonelle's *Dictate Your Book* has a lot of great tips on dictation and when I interviewed her, she noted,

> "Dragon thinks very differently than we do. **We think in words, but Dragon thinks in phrases.** So think about what you're going to say and then speak it with confidence. This makes punctuation easier too."

This is a really good tip and why I use the pause button when dictating. Dragon and other speech recognition software use placement and order because **language is not just about an individual word, it's about context**. This is really important. When you're typing, you think about each word, whereas when you're dictating, you need to speak in phrases.

Productivity and habits are different for everyone and you have to find the way that works for you. Scott Baker, author of *The Writer's Guide to Training Your Dragon* talks about this in more detail.

> "**Embrace dictation as a productivity tool.** It's a weapon in your writing arsenal and your workflow.
>
> Don't treat it like it's something completely alien. We're familiar with the keyboard, but that isn't necessarily the best input method anyway. Input methods keep changing. We've had the quill, and then we had the pen, and then we have the typewriter, and now we have the computer keyboard. In the last few years, we've had touch.
>
> I genuinely believe that the next big input method is voice. **In the next 10 years, if you're not embracing voice, you will be behind in the same way as if you don't have a smartphone right now.** You're missing out on a lot of technological help."

I also recommend *Fool Proof Dictation* by Christopher Downing, where he stresses the importance of warming up and cyclical dictation exercises that lead up to the main dictation session. He also stresses quality and a cleaner first draft with this cycling approach.

"If we can get high words and yet, at the same time, warm up the craft side of our brain where we can dictate a decent sentence, or a somewhat complicated sentence that's written beautifully, I think that this is better in the end."

You can listen to all these interviews and find more options for dictation at:

TheCreativePenn.com/dictation

All these books and interviews are useful, but at some point, you need to try dictation yourself. Open one of the free options and record a few paragraphs. Pick some of your own text or take a book off the shelf and read it aloud. You might find that dictation is the tool that transforms your writing productivity.

* * *

Questions:

- Why might you consider dictation? How might it help your writing?

- What's stopping you from dictating? How can you work through those issues in order to try it?

- What method of dictation might work for you?

- What tools do you need to get started?

9. Co-writing and collaboration

Co-writing is a great way to be more productive and has become common among indie authors writing fiction and non-fiction series in the last few years.

I've co-written seven books at this point, including *Risen Gods* and *Co-Writing a Book* with J. Thorn. We updated the latter after we took the train from Chicago to New Orleans with Zach Bohannon and Lindsay Buroker and co-wrote *American Demon Hunters: Sacrifice* together. I've also co-written *The Healthy Writer* with Dr. Euan Lawson and three Summerfield Village sweet romance books with my mum under the pen-name, Penny Appleton.

I have no doubt that I will co-write more in my career, so why might you consider co-writing?

Faster production

It's intoxicating just how fast you can produce a first draft when two (or more) people write together. When J and I wrote *Risen Gods*, I was in the UK and he was in Ohio, USA. I would get up and write first thing in my morning, and by the time J got up five hours later, I'd already written 2,000 words. He would pick up the draft and write another 2,000 words. Working at that pace, we finished the first draft in just over three weeks and the workload was far less than doing it alone.

Original creativity

There is no way I would have written *The Healthy Writer* without co-writing with a medical doctor. The book was Euan's idea and together, we wrote something that would not have existed otherwise and that has helped a lot of writers. Euan could not have written a self-help book of that kind without me and I certainly would not have written a health book without him. It's a perfect example of a book that needed to exist and would not have happened without the magic of co-writing.

Risen Gods is set in New Zealand. The original idea was mine because I lived there for a long time and I wanted to write something about Maori gods in the aftermath of the earthquakes that devastated Christchurch in 2011. I could have written it alone, but together, J and I turned the novel into something far more. The whole is definitely greater than the sum of its parts when it comes to co-writing.

Camaraderie

For *American Demon Hunters: Sacrifice*, the four of us took the train from Chicago to New Orleans and then stayed a week to write the first draft together. We explored the city after our writing sessions so it was a lot of fun as well as challenging to weave our different writing styles together into a coherent narrative.

I co-wrote with my mum to help her move into writing at a later stage of her life. We started on the first Penny Appleton sweet romance, *Love, Second Time Around*, when she was 68 and she's now in her 70s and loving her writing career.

Marketing

If you co-write with authors in the same niche, there will be opportunities to market the books together and bring new readers into your eco-system. It also shares the load of a necessary part of the process that few writers love.

* * *

So if co-writing is so great, why isn't everyone doing it? What are the difficulties with co-writing?

Creative differences

With *American Demon Hunters: Sacrifice*, we had four independent writers co-writing one story. It was one of the hardest things I've ever had to do creatively because we are very different writers. For example, Lindsay Buroker, who is an incredible fantasy author, writes 100,000-word fantasy novels every month. She writes long, I write short. She's funny, I'm serious. Zach and J also write in different voices, so it was a challenge to work together, especially with only one week for a first draft.

After much story wrangling, we decided to write separate chapters in the voices of four different characters and knit the story together that way. It was a great experience, but certainly a challenge!

Compromise

When you're working with someone else, you have to compromise. This was hard with my mum as we're both strong characters. The books were in her voice and she wrote the first draft but, as I'm the more experienced writer, there were definitely occasions where I had to take the lead. We did three books together and then parted ways as co-writers. This is common among co-writers and of course, she's my mum, so we parted amicably.

> If you'd like to listen to a discussion of what worked and why we decided to stop co-writing together, listen at TheCreativePenn.com/penny

Unequal partnerships

Co-writing can work well if you bring different skills, but massive inequality can also make it difficult. On *The Healthy Writer*, our respective differences worked well. Euan is a medical doctor and I've written lots of books, so we brought different strengths. Euan was excellent at writing for medical journals, but he had to relax his style to write for a general audience. He didn't have a way to market the book, whereas I brought over a decade of The Creative Penn community to the mix.

It was particularly difficult with my mum because she'd never written a book before. The difference in our awareness around writing was challenging, and she also didn't want to do any marketing. I did those three books out of love and I'm grateful that I had the chance to help her, but I would not repeat the experience with a new writer again.

If you understand your differences going in, then co-writing can work well, but if you don't realize them until later, it can be a challenge.

Payment splitting

Post-publication, you will have to split royalties for the life of the book, which could be the rest of your life and 50 to 70 years after you die according to the term of copyright, unless you un-publish it earlier.

There should be a spike in income on release, but inevitably, income per book goes down over time (unless you keep marketing) and some of those payments might only be a few dollars. You can use services like Publish Drive's Abacus or BundleRabbit's Collaboration Engine to split payments, or of course, you can do it manually on a spreadsheet, but you have to do it somehow.

* * *

I definitely don't want to put you off co-writing. In fact, I would encourage it, but in very specific situations. What can you do to increase your chances of success?

Pick the right partner

If you want to be productive with co-writing, you need the right partner, because otherwise you might be dragging them along or they might be dragging you along. This is where the inequality aspect comes in, so do your due diligence around who you co-write with.

Make sure you write in compatible genres

You might be at a similar level in terms of writing experience, and even in terms of marketing platform, but if you write in completely different genres, it's going to be difficult and your books won't cross-sell either. You can respect each other as writers, but that's not the only reason for co-writing together.

Use a written contract

Copyright lasts longer than a marriage. It lasts after your death. So you have to talk about serious things if you co-write a book. What happens if one of you dies? What happens if you have incredible success like a movie deal? What happens if it is an utter failure and a waste of time and money? If you talk about this upfront, you're going to make the whole process a lot easier, and if you write it all down, then you have a framework you don't have to argue about later.

You also need to establish how you're going to work together. For example, how much time you will each spend writing, your timeline, target word count and how you're going to split the publishing and marketing process if you're self-publishing. Who's going to pay for editing, cover design, and marketing tasks?

This upfront communication will help you to work out whether or not you want to take your relationship into co-writing, and stop the process early if you find it's not going to work out.

Trust and honest, regular, transparent communication

If you pick a partner who doesn't communicate, it's not going to work, but you don't have to actually 'talk' to each other. J and I didn't. We used a Google Doc and left each other notes every day. We would write our words, then we would write our comments. We did pretty much everything without speaking because we're both introverts and prefer written communication. Once you start writing, you need to communicate about the writing process itself and share your draft work in progress.

You also need to encourage each other. Some days, one of you will write 3,000 words and the other one will write 500 words, or maybe nothing at all. You don't want resentment or bad feelings to build up. We all have up and down days, we all have creative differences. You need to trust the other person in terms of emotional support and also trust them to read your first draft. I was most nervous about that aspect with J, as no one had ever read my first draft before, but when you're co-writing, you need to **leave your ego at the door** because no one's first draft is perfect!

After publication, you still need to communicate throughout the publishing and ongoing marketing process as well as for payment splitting.

Practicalities of co-writing

Outlining really helps, otherwise you will end up wasting time. I remember one night in New Orleans, J and Zach, Lindsay and I had to sit down and thrash out the story. We had not outlined it enough to understand where everyone was going with their individual character arcs, and as a discovery writer, I found that aspect challenging. It was the fourth day of a seven-day writing trip so we had to sort it out in order to finish the book on time. We replanned everything, but once we had the outline, we all wrote much faster and in a more coherent way.

Google Docs is the most common tool for co-writing. It's free and you can just share your documents with the other person. Some authors use a Scrivener project synced through Dropbox but you need to be careful not to overwrite the other person's work. There are other collaboration tools like StoryShop.io, so you can choose what works best for you.

I have always used Google Docs and at the end of the first draft, I copy and paste all of the chapters into Scrivener and do the first editing pass before handing it over to my co-writer for the next round of edits.

* * *

This is just an overview of the co-writing process, so if you want more information and details of contracts and working together, then check out, *Co-Writing A Book: Collaboration and Co-creation for Writers* by Joanna Penn and J. Thorn.

Questions:

- Why do you want to co-write or collaborate with another writer? What are the pros and cons for you?

- Why are you a good fit as a partnership?

- Have you laid out working process, deadlines, money, etc., in a written document?

- How will you make sure that your collaboration works for the long term?

10. Outsourcing

Outsourcing plays an important part in productivity. We want to spend our precious time on the things that take us toward our goals, but there are always other tasks that need to be done, and those can be outsourced.

If you're at the beginning of your author journey, you might not think outsourcing is applicable to you, but it's important to consider because at some point, you're going to realize that you want some of your time back and you're willing to pay for help.

If you're further on in your writing career, this may be the most important chapter, because outsourcing is the only way you can achieve more in a creative business. Many people ask how I get so much done as an author entrepreneur, and although I do manage my time well, these days it's all about automation of tasks and outsourcing to skilled freelancers.

If you want to be a successful author, you will need help at some point on the journey

I resisted this for a long time. For the first five years of my author business, I did pretty much everything myself. I did hire freelance editors and cover designers but I learned how to build and manage my website, podcast and book marketing as well as all the other technical elements required for self-publishing. Part of that was due to budget, because I bootstrapped my business while working my day job, but I also felt the need to control everything and I was sure that no one else could do what I did as well as I could.

But over time, I found myself getting more and more overwhelmed. I didn't have time to do everything. I was writing more books, podcasting every week, blogging and running the business as well as speaking professionally, plus trying to exercise and maintain a happy marriage. My income had plateaued because I didn't have enough time to work *on* the business as well as *in* the business. There were many aspects that had begun to feel like a job and I was on the edge of burn-out. Not what I imagined for my creative career. I didn't have the extra money to outsource, but I knew I needed to find it to save my sanity.

Perhaps you know how this feels?

How could you automate or outsource tasks to free up your time?

As an example of what this might look like, here's my team right now. I work with several different editors and a cover designer who is also my graphic designer. My fantastic virtual assistant, Alexandra, takes care of content for my main websites and manages guest posting and transcript formatting for the podcast. I also have a freelance writer for articles on my site, BooksAndTravel.page, and I have an audio engineer for my podcast and audiobooks. I use a transcription service and my husband, Jonathan, does my Amazon advertising. I use a premium hosting service, WP Engine, so I have fewer maintenance issues with my website, as well as a great accountant.

My most recent team member is Carly, my inbox manager for The Creative Penn email account, which gets really busy every day with questions from writers. I only made that change in January 2019 because I was spending 8-10 hours a week doing email. I love helping people but something had to give! Carly does the triage and I answer anything personal or complicated, or anything from my Patrons on Patreon. So, if you are a member of my community, don't worry, I am still here!

> "It's better to disappoint a few people over small things than to surrender your dreams for an empty inbox."
>
> Jocelyn K. Glei, *Manage Your Day-To-Day*

All these people are freelancers except for my husband, Jonathan. We are both directors and employees of the business, but everyone else is a freelancer, so the hours worked are a **scalable expense** depending on what people are needed for. It's taken time to find the right people, but it's made all the difference to my productivity and my happiness.

If you find the idea of outsourcing difficult, think about it in terms of productivity. How do you define a productive and successful author? How do you measure that? If it's number of books written and published or number of books sold or income made per month, how do you give yourself more time to do that? Outsourcing is often the answer.

If you're struggling with what to outsource, it's time for self-examination.

Which zone are you working in most of the time?

I highly recommend reading *The Big Leap* by Gay Hendricks, which talks about four different zones:

Zone of Incompetence: You're not good at this. Many other people can do this better.

Zone of Competence: You can do this but others can do it better.

Zone of Excellence: You're skilled in this area and not many others can do it like you can.

Zone of Genius: No one else can do this but you.

Think about each of these zones for your situation and reflect on how you're spending your precious time. Here are my examples.

Zone of Incompetence

I need an editor. I'm not 'incompetent' at self-editing, but I always need to work with an editor and I always have. Editing is definitely not my job, neither is proofreading, book cover design, graphic design, bookkeeping or accounting. Other people do those things well, so I definitely outsource those.

Zone of Competence

I format my ebooks with Vellum. It's so easy and I love it so I'll continue to do that. But formatting print books is not my job, because I'm just not detail orientated enough. I've tried in the past and I've done a mediocre job. So, I outsource print formatting. I can do audio editing and podcast production. I did it for years, but others are better than me. The same applies to formatting blog posts. I can do that, but should I be spending my time on that now? No, so my virtual assistant, Alexandra, does that for me and does a wonderful job.

Zone of Excellence

I'm a professional speaker. I've been paid to speak all over the world in the last decade and I get good feedback from my events. But although I continue to speak occasionally, I don't want my business to revolve around speaking. That's not what I want to do with my life so it will only be occasional in the future.

Zone of Genius

I struggled with the word 'genius' at first. I thought "I'm not a genius at anything." But it's more about what you bring to the world that no one else can. That's what you should be spending your time on.

For me, it's writing my books, both fiction and non-fiction, as well as podcasting. No one else has my personal experiences to share. No one else can write the books I write. No one else can podcast in the way that I do. Podcasting and voice are so intimate. It has to be my voice in your head. I also love to create in the written and audio formats.

So, writing and podcasting are aspects within my Zone of Genius, which is where I should be spending my time.

> **Sometimes you have to give up areas of Competence and Excellence in order to make time for your Zone of Genius.**

Complete this exercise for your own situation. Are you spending more time in other zones than in your Zone of Genius? What can you do to focus on the things that only you can do?

This reframing of activities can help you to change the way you spend your time. Remember, **productivity is about focusing on the things that you *should* be doing** instead of filling your time with stuff that you shouldn't be doing.

What about the money?

Paying for business tools and outsourcing is a challenge, but take it slow and make changes over time. You don't have to do it all at once. I added new people into my team as I earned more money, reinvesting in order to buy more time.

Bootstrap at the beginning, do it yourself, but put some money away, start saving from your royalties or your day job or whatever else is funding your life. As your income grows, you can invest in learning more skills but also in outsourcing tasks to others.

It's a false economy to do everything yourself, so think about it as an investment. Give yourself more time to create.

Ready to outsource?
Follow these 8 steps

One of the biggest mistakes with outsourcing is trying to hire one person to do everything you can't or don't want to do. Chris Ducker, in his great book *Virtual Freedom: How to Work with Virtual Staff to Buy More Time, Become More Productive, and Build Your Dream Business.* addresses the **myth of the 'super VA,'** the idea that you can hire someone just like you.

It's much better to work with people within *their* Zone of Excellence or Genius. For example, I wouldn't use the same freelancer to design my book covers as I would to fix my WordPress website, or try and convince a fiction editor to work on editing my audiobooks. Keep this in mind as you go through the steps.

(1) Make a list of everything you do currently

If you are going ahead with outsourcing, then start by making a list of everything you do and group it into logical tasks. This is not so much your 'To Do' list but more the repetitive tasks that occur within your author business in each cycle of creativity.

Many authors think, "Oh, I'll just get someone to do my marketing." But 'marketing' is a catch-all word, so you need to be more specific. For example, you might want someone to create infographics for Pinterest, or a freelance writer to create content for your blog, or someone to pitch book review bloggers and podcasters, or someone to schedule your Facebook posts. Each of these is a different task, so write down whatever you have on your list.

(2) Eliminate items from your list. What really needs doing?

Remember the quote from Gretchen Rubin, "The biggest waste of time is to do well something that we need not do at all."

We started on elimination in Chapter 5 but now you need to go through the list again, because this time you will be paying someone else to do it. Do you *really* want to pay a virtual assistant \$20-\$40 an hour to schedule your Twitter stream or create shareable images for your blog when you have no traffic or income?

This is why most authors start with outsourcing the necessary tasks of editing and book cover design and then add aspects like building a website and setting up an email list before social media scheduling and marketing tasks.

(3) Write procedures or record videos of your current process

When I handed over my podcast production, I recorded a video of how I did the process at the time and indicated that change would be fine as long as we achieved the same or a better result. When I handed over my Inbox for The Creative Penn, I created a multi-page document with all the most common questions and appropriate answers so responding would be easier.

At this point, you might also consider automation. For example, I used to update plugins manually on my Word-Press sites and considered outsourcing as it is a regular and repetitive task. But quotes were always high for what is generally a basic activity. Then my hosting service, WPEngine, introduced a tool that did this automatically which I immediately purchased, saving me from both manual work and the need to outsource.

The main thing to decide is whether to eliminate a task completely, automate it or write out a procedure and outsource it.

(4) Find virtual assistants and freelancers

Try the author community first. I found my wonderful virtual assistant, Alexandra, and my audio engineer, Dan, by asking for help on my podcast. They emailed me and that's how we ended up working together. I met my book cover designer, Jane, at an author event in the UK and now she's an important member of my extended freelance team. I joined InboxDone through Yaro Starak, who taught me about online business through his Blog Profits Blueprint, and started the company to help entrepreneurs like me.

You can find people in the same way. Maybe you're in an author Facebook group, or you could become a member of the Alliance of Independent Authors which has a partner member network. Find people you trust and ask for referrals.

> Another good place to start is Reedsy which you can find at TheCreativePenn.com/reedsy

They have vetted professionals including editors, marketers, book cover designers, ghostwriters, website help, and all kinds of other freelancers who specialize in working with authors. You can also look at wider freelance networks like Upwork.com.

If you want to offer your services to authors, then I recommend applying to the Alliance of Independent Authors Partner Member list and also working with Reedsy, because then people know you've been vetted.

The following lists are made up of members from my community or recommended by them:

- Editors: TheCreativePenn.com/editors
- Book Cover Designers: TheCreativePenn.com/bookcoverdesign
- Formatting: TheCreativePenn.com/formatting

Please note that I have not worked with everyone on these lists personally so please do your due diligence.

(5) Interview first

Once you find a potential freelancer, you need to know whether you can work together, especially when trust is involved around access to specific things like your website or inbox. You could do a Skype interview, or if you're a serious introvert, you could always live chat or email, but it is important to set expectations and discover whether you will be able to work together.

Trust is so important to me because I've spent over a decade building my business and it's my income, my reputation and everything I have created. I don't give anyone my Amazon login, my PayPal login, or access to my bank account, but clearly I am sharing access to my website and inbox which are sensitive. You can use services like Last-Pass.com to share logins and keep things partially secure, but at the end of the day, you have to find people you can trust, and interviewing is a key part of that.

(6) Communicate expectations upfront and stay in touch

Once you've interviewed someone and you both decide to move forward, then **make sure you document how you're going to work together,** your respective responsibilities, communication, billing, updates and anything else.

A simple contract is the best thing to have with any free-lancer. Many freelancers will have their own contracts, but if they don't, you can document everything you've agreed and both sign it. Obviously, I'm not a lawyer and if you want to get legal help for specific contracts, then go ahead.

In terms of tools, I use Google Drive and Dropbox for sharing and working together on documents. I pay all my freelancers by PayPal if they are overseas or bank transfer if they are in the UK. You can use LastPass to share pass-words with other people.

I would recommend starting with a small project, like a single article for your blog, or editing one chapter, or scheduling social media for a week in order to test out the process before committing for a longer period. This will enable you to build up trust over time.

(7) Be a good client

If you want great freelancers, then you need to be a good client. I pay immediately on receipt of invoice because I want my wonderful freelancers to love working with me. I want to be one of their top clients, so I respect their skills, I let them do their work, thank them and pay quickly.

The best freelancers have a choice of people they can work with, so if you're not a good client, they will find other work. Give constructive feedback, be positive, respect their expertise and, most importantly, pay on time.

You're using *their* brain and *their* time instead of yours. This is why outsourcing is a secret weapon for productivity. Of course, they're going to do things differently than you and they may well do it better. You can coach them if they are not doing things exactly as you like, but often, they're going to be completely fine doing things on their own. That's the point of outsourcing!

(8) Communicate

Communicate regularly in an open and honest way and beware of extended periods of non-response or silence. This could indicate trouble, so protect yourself and make sure you back everything important up regularly. Make sure you know how to revoke access and change passwords if necessary.

Be ready to let the freelancer go if things don't work. Early on in my outsourcing process, I tried to hire someone to do everything and inevitably we both ended up disappointed. Another time, I tried to negotiate a contract with a free-lancer who took it the wrong way and we parted ways even before we started. This is just part of the process. Maybe you just don't work well together, maybe it's just the time is up. These things happen.

There are inevitable risks with opening up your processes and I understand the difficulties in letting things go, but you have to, or you'll never escape overwhelm, be more productive and grow your author business.

* * *

Questions:

- Do you currently work with different freelancers? How much do you do yourself? How much do you WANT to do yourself?

- What are your zones of incompetence, competence, excellence and genius? Are you spending too much time in the wrong zone?

- What is stopping you from hiring more help right now? How can you remedy that so you have more time to create?

- Make a list of everything you do, and split it into logical groupings

- Eliminate tasks that really don't need doing – or don't need doing right now

- Could any of the tasks be automated?

- Where can you look for freelancers or virtual assistants? How will you work effectively with them?

11. Productivity tools

These are some of the tools that I use for productivity but of course, you don't need to use all of them!

If you have a problem they might solve, then by all means, go ahead. But sometimes we can use new technology to procrastinate so be aware of what you really need and only add tools when you are ready.

Back up your writing

You can't be productive if you lose your work or if you're disorganized with your manuscript.

I still hear surprisingly often from people who have lost drafts because they didn't back up their writing. I've never lost a draft (touch wood!) because I back up my writing after every session, so I hope that it will never happen to me, but it's definitely one of those things that can occur unless you are careful.

Keep all the different versions of your work

I write in Scrivener but every single day I write, I compile a MSWord document of my work in progress (WIP). I save it with a date and time stamp and keep all the iterations, so I end up with a Draft folder with 50+ documents in.

This is called **version control.** If you haven't worked in the corporate or tech world, you might not know about version control, but basically, even if I lose one of these versions, I've got so many others over time that I will never lose everything. I don't go back and look at those older drafts but if something happens, I won't lose the whole project.

I also email the file to myself every day on Gmail so I always have another backup and I save the Draft to a Dropbox folder in the cloud which syncs between workstations. Even if my MacBook Pro gets stolen or blows up, everything is in Dropbox.

I do this for every writing session, whether it's first draft or editing. Every time I touch the manuscript, I compile it, save it to Dropbox, and email it to myself. Sometimes that is two or three times a day during my intensive writing phases.

I also keep backups on physical external hard drives and save some important files to Amazon S3 cloud hosting, so I back up pretty much everything multiple times to build in redundancy. I worked in the tech industry for 13 years, so I know these things are necessary and saving too much is better than losing it all.

Organize your computer file structure

Do you have an organized way of finding your work in progress on your computer? Or do you have a multitude of files on your desktop and in your download folder and tons of miscellaneous documents cluttering up your creative digital space?

You might be able to get away with being disorganized when you have one book, but trust me, when you have lots of them in multiple formats and maybe even multiple languages over time, you need a file structure you can easily navigate.

My file structure has the following hierarchy:

- **Author name:** I have folders for Joanna Penn (non-fiction for authors), and J.F.Penn (thrillers and dark fantasy)

- **Status:** Completed, In Progress, To Write, Other Stuff

- **Series:** This is mainly for my fiction, for example, ARKANE, London Crime Thrillers, Mapwalkers, Standalones

- **Book title:** This is a folder for everything to do with the book

- Within the book folder, I'll keep the Master Scrivener project and a Drafts folder when starting out and over time, I'll add folders for the **cover and different formats, marketing materials** and even screen prints of ranking success

The file structure is the same for every book so I don't have to spend time looking for things when I need them. My business is more than just books so I have other hierarchies for the podcast, licensing under my publishing imprint, Curl Up Press, and more. Everything has its place.

If your file structure isn't organized right now, this is something you definitely need to make time for. Bite the bullet, go a little Marie Kondo, declutter and organize things and you will find everything is easier over time.

If you have items you don't know what to do with, I tend to put things in a Miscellaneous, deal-with-later folder. I'll go in there occasionally and delete all the old stuff that I haven't opened for years.

Calendar

I run my life on Google Calendar. I used a physical Filofax organizer for many years, but switching to Google Calendar has definitely made me more productive. It's on my phone and laptop and I plan my weeks in detail but also have recurring time blocks, sometimes for months or even years into the future. For example, my morning writing time is a recurring slot.

This is how I get everything done. I make the time, I put the blocks into my calendar and then I show up for those appointments with myself.

I make sure that every working day has some kind of asset creation or income-producing activity. My writing time is definitely asset creation, because once the finished book goes out into the world, I know it will make money. Recording and editing audiobooks is also about creating another intellectual property asset, and my podcasts are both income-producing and marketing, and I consider them part of my body of work so those activities have specific time slots.

I schedule yoga and other classes for health, my long Sunday walks, and also recurring life admin tasks that we all have to do like paying the credit card bill or doing accounting.

I use Calendly for scheduling my podcast interviews, which has definitely saved time. Before using it, I emailed backward and forward with interview guests to find a time that worked in their time zone and mine, but Calendly just syncs with my Google Calendar and they can pick a time that works for us both. If you schedule interviews or arrange time with other people, Calendly is really useful.

To Do list

I use the Things app every day. It really is my external brain and one of the first things I open every morning. It holds my reminders, recurring tasks, and To Do list for the short term and long term with dates for when they pop up. I keep template emails there and also have a fiction folder for logging random ideas or quotes that I like.

Things is Mac-only and syncs between my phone and laptop. It doesn't matter what To Do app you use but you need to use something. You can't keep everything in your brain or on bits of paper. Have a look at the options and find one that works for you.

Scrivener

Scrivener is my favorite writing productivity tool, and in my *How to Write a Novel* and *How to Write Non-Fiction* courses, I go into how I use it for pre-writing, organizing, plotting and also for writing and tracking.

In terms of productivity, I use two specific aspects:

Project Targets: Set your Project Goals based on overall word count, days you will write and your deadline and Scrivener will calculate your **Session Target**: The number of words you need to write per session in order to achieve your goal. It's helpful to see the progress bar turn from red to green every time you write.

Flags: I use flags as a visual aid to measure progress. When I've finished a chapter in my first draft, I add a yellow flag. When all chapters have yellow flags, I've finished a first draft. I'll print out the draft and then edit by hand.

After editing, I update Scrivener with the changes and turn the flag blue. I might do another editing pass and change the flag color again and then when the manuscript is finished, I'll turn the flags green. That's when I export out of Scrivener to MS Word in order to send to my editor.

Password protection and management

Like most people, I used to use the same few passwords on every site, but that's just not a good idea when even the biggest sites get hacked. I now use 1Password for the business and personal passwords and LastPass to share passwords with freelancers.

You can **create secure passwords** without having to make them up yourself and save them in a vault. All you have to remember is one master password.

You can also **share vaults.** My husband, Jonathan, and I work on things together within the business so we share a log-on for certain sites. You can secure your personal passwords and share others.

Dropbox

Dropbox is great for collaboration and keeping your work in the cloud. They have a business account if you need extra features. My husband and I have a shared business drive and I have separate shared drives with my virtual assistants for different aspects of work. I also have a temporary folder where I keep things I know I will delete later, for example, recordings from interviews.

If you run an online, location-independent business, you need something like Dropbox to keep your work in the cloud. You could use Google Drive or Amazon Drive or another service but don't keep everything on one computer, as you risk losing it all if something goes wrong technically.

Evernote

I use Evernote as a place to put articles I find for various things. I have folders for maps and cartography, a folder for The Creative Penn, a folder for fiction thoughts and ideas and interesting stuff. I save useful articles from Feedly (which aggregates blog articles) into an Evernote shared folder and then Alexandra, my virtual assistant, will go in and schedule them into my social media feeds.

Many authors use Evernote far more extensively than I do and if you go down the Evernote rabbit-hole, you can find lots more applications that might be useful.

Social media scheduling

If you follow me on Twitter, you might think I'm on there 24/7, but mainly it's all scheduled and I only check it a couple of times per day. My Facebook is also scheduled, but I do Instagram @jfpennauthor myself, as that is more personal.

Scheduling is the key to social media if you want an active presence but you don't want to be on it all the time. I use BufferApp.com as my main scheduling tool. You can set up a timetable and load content that will post at specific times.

Missinglettr.com is also good for generating a series of tweets from one blog post and then scheduling them across a timeline.

Some authors recommend IFTTT.com which stands for If This Then That, and this is a rule-based system that can help your workflow. You can also use Later.com for Instagram in particular. Zapier.com can also help you link tasks between applications.

Email list management

It's important to have something that helps you work quickly and easily for email marketing and I really like ConvertKit. Over the last decade, I've used AWeber and then ActiveCampaign, but ConvertKit is designed for creatives running an online business so I find it works best for me.

ConvertKit has made me more productive with email because, honestly, I don't hate doing it so much! It's easy to set up and use, which is important, because I definitely resist email marketing but I have to do it because it's an important part of running an online business.

I have a tutorial here on how to set up your email list with ConvertKit:

TheCreativePenn.com/setup-email-list

Teachable for online courses

Many authors use teaching for another stream of income and if you want to teach online, I recommend Teachable for hosting and managing the payment and taxes.

Over the last decade teaching online, I've used lots of different technical solutions but Teachable is my preferred option. They host the video and audio files and deal with payments, digital taxes and affiliate management. It's a fantastic service and very reasonably priced.

Check it out at TheCreativePenn.com/teachable

Accounting and bookkeeping

Many authors start out with spreadsheets but over time, if your business becomes more significant, you'll need accounting software, bookkeeping help and maybe even an accountant.

I use Xero for my accounting software which integrates with my bank statement and PayPal as well as importing credit card statements for reconciliation. Other options include Freshbooks or QuickBooks which have similar functionality. I also work with an accountant for my taxes as I run a Limited Company in the UK.

Stop distraction with Freedom

If you're struggling with distraction and you're checking social media too much during your writing sessions, then try the Freedom app on your phone.

As Julia Cameron says, **"It is a paradox that by emptying our lives of distractions we are actually filling the well."**

Keep that in mind, because I don't want you to fill your writing life with a load of new tools! Use those that will help but only when you need them.

* * *

Questions:

- Is there a part of your process that could be improved with a tool?

- Which tool/s could help you to become more productive?

12. The productive writer mindset

This is just an overview on mindset as it relates to productivity. For more detail, check out *The Successful Author Mindset*, also available as a Workbook edition.

Be self-aware

One of the most important mindset shifts is being totally honest and aware of what is *really* stopping you from being productive. Once you uncover the root cause, then you can start to fix it.

Self-awareness means that you need to spend some time digging into your motivations. Keep asking why.

For example, let's take the most common issue cited by those who want to write a book but can't seem to achieve that goal: "I don't have the time to write."

We all have the same 24 hours in a day, so what underlies this lack of time?

Perhaps you feel guilty about spending time on your writing when you need to be making money or spending time with your family. Perhaps you're not willing to give up your TV or gaming habit to write. Perhaps you don't really want to write a book, you just want to talk about writing. Perhaps you're afraid of failure if it doesn't work out?

These may sound harsh, but something has to underlie the lack of time, so what is it for you?

Here are some other common issues.

"I don't want to schedule my time. That's not very creative."

Some writers think that scheduling time to create is too rigid because they can only write when the muse alights and when they're in flow.

But that's not the reality of being a writer.

As Stephen King says in *On Writing*, "Don't wait for the muse."

It's easier to create within boundaries, and you're already setting specific boundaries for your book, so why is time any different? For example, is it too rigid to decide to write a non-fiction book about gut health or a historical romance set in 19th-century America? The more boundaries you set, the easier it is to create.

Use a schedule and boundaries to create more effectively

If you haven't tried scheduling your writing time slots and you're not productive enough, then get on with it. Stop making excuses. Why wouldn't you try it for a month and see if it works? It's a bit like any new way of eating or a new form of exercise. It doesn't work if you only do it twice and then give up. But if you are consistent over time, the process will work.

So, give it a try, schedule your writing time for a month, and see if you get a lot more done than you did when you just waited for inspiration.

> "Great creative minds think like artists
> but work like accountants."
>
> Cal Newport, *Deep Work*

Time and quality

Some writers think that it should take a long time to write a 'quality' book and more productive writers must be inferior in some way because they produce more quickly. But there are several aspects to this.

Most authors have a full-time job and write on the side. Very few authors are truly full-time, and those who are tend to be prolific. Consider Nora Roberts, one of the most-loved and highest-earning authors in the world, appearing on the Forbes Richest Author list most years. Nora writes a book every 45 days and has won pretty much every award there is for her books.

For those of a literary persuasion, Charles Dickens took six weeks to write *A Christmas Carol*. R.L.Stevenson wrote *Dr. Jekyll and Mr. Hyde* in a week. Ray Bradbury spent nine days on *Fahrenheit 451*.

Self-publishing has enabled many authors to write at speed and produce books faster than ever before. But this is all just math. If you spend 8-10 hours a day on your book and you write 10,000 words a day, you will be faster at producing a first draft than someone only writing five hours a week. Time elapsed is not the same as time spent on a book.

It also depends on the length of your book. *Dr. Jekyll and Mr. Hyde* and *Fahrenheit 451* are practically novellas compared to today's bestsellers, and many famous literary novels are short. You don't have to write 120,000 words to create a book that satisfies readers.

The definition of quality is also different for every person, and each reader will judge quality when they read. I often download a sample of ebooks I'm interested in. If I don't like the book within a couple of pages, I just delete it. If I read to the end of the sample, I will often buy immediately. I judge quality on how much I want to keep reading. I don't care how long it took to write.

In the end, you can't judge quality or reader satisfaction by the time it takes to write a book, so don't let this mindset issue stop you from being more productive.

Writer's block

Writer's block is not a single monolithic issue. It has different aspects and different causes, depending on where you are in your author journey, your life, and the creative process.

One possible issue for new writers is that **you don't know enough about the process of writing**. If you need help with the craft side, there are myriad books on all aspects of writing and I also have courses on *How to Write a Novel* and *How to Write Non-Fiction*.

Another possible block is that **you've run out of ideas.** Maybe you don't know what's going to happen next in a novel. Or you only have two chapters in your non-fiction book and don't know what else to write.

The answer is to fill the creative well. Read some books or watch documentaries or movies about the topic or in the genre. Go to a museum or art gallery. Listen to podcasts or interview some experts. Get away from the page and you will find inspiration.

Of course, you should never copy, plagiarize or steal other people's ideas, but you can twist existing ideas into something new. That's the essence of creativity, so you need that underlying material in order to form your own.

Writing is hard

Sometimes when people say they have a 'block,' it's because they still believe the myth that writing comes easy, that you just sit down, enter a flow state and perfection will stream from your fingers.

But that's just not true, and if you want to be productive as a writer, you need to acknowledge that it is work like any other work. It's very satisfying to write and I love what I do. I measure my life by what I create and at this point, I expect to be writing books until I die — but it's not easy. You have to be willing to do the work.

So, how much do you want this? How much do you want to hold your book in your hand? If you want to take it further, how much do you want to make a living from your writing?

> "Talent is cheaper than table salt.
> What separates the talented individual from
> the successful one is a lot of hard work."
>
> Stephen King, *On Writing*

"I feel guilty because I'm not writing."

This is a surprisingly common issue. We all have complicated lives, and we all need to make time and space for writing. But if you have made time and space for your writing and you have your setup in place, and you're *still* not writing, then you need to examine why.

Have you skipped multiple writing sessions in a row?

How many have you missed?

Is there a good reason why you've missed them?

If you are really sick, stop worrying and rest. Some people do write when they're sick, others don't. Be gentle with yourself, understand that there are seasons of life and everything gets complicated at some point.

But if you *have* made time and space and there's no good reason for skipping the writing sessions, then **what else is going on?**

This is where it comes back to self-awareness. For example, maybe you're afraid of it. Maybe you're in love with the *idea* of writing, but you don't actually want to write.

I was in that space for years before I sat down and did the work. If you're struggling with this, then I'd suggest timed writing or booking a course in person that will force you over that hump. Or find an accountability partner, meet a local friend at the library or café or something, and then write. Don't chat.

If there's a good reason you haven't been writing, don't feel guilty, just take action.

Self-doubt

This common issue comes in many forms. "X writer is better than me, I'll never be that good. I'll never win that prize, so what's the point? What if my books don't sell? What if I don't get an agent? What is the point of writing when I know I'm going to fail?"

All of these things will come up over and over again. If you're struggling with this aspect, in particular, check out *The Successful Author Mindset,* which covers self-doubt, fear of failure, fear of judgment (one of my big issues), and a whole load of other things that are part of the creative process.

I constantly feel like I'm not good enough. I read Stephen King and wonder why I even bother to try.

Then, I remember that Stephen King started writing early with his first rejection slip at 14. He's in his seventies as I write this, at least 25 years older than me and I only started writing at 32. So he has more than 40 years' more experience than I do and a lot more books under his belt.

The only way for me to become a writer like King — and even if you don't like his books, you've got to admit, he's a great writing role model — is to keep writing and keep learning and improving.

Revisit your why and use that reason to drive you back to the page. Have a cry if you need to, moan to your friends and then do the work.

Comparing yourself to other authors can be dangerous, but it can also help you to identify what you are aiming at, as with my example with King above. Who do you compare yourself to and why?

The other trick is to **compare yourself to yourself** six

months ago, or a year ago, or even ten years ago. A decade ago, I had just started writing my first novel. I had a fledgling website and podcast with no income from my writing at all. I worked for a mining company in Australia implementing an Accounts Payable IT solution. I could not have imagined where I would be ten years later.

Reflect on your journey. What were you doing this time last year? Or five years ago. What have you achieved toward your writing goals? How far have you come? If you haven't achieved a lot, why not? What can you do to make sure you don't feel the same next year?

* * *

These are just some of the mindset issues you might face as a writer. Don't worry! You're not alone. These are all common within the author community and in fact, you might face them with every creative project. You just have to learn to incorporate them and deal with each as it arises.

It all comes down to self-awareness and finding what works for you.

"We won't make ourselves more creative and productive by copying other people's habits, even the habits of geniuses. We must know our own nature and what habits serve us best."

Gretchen Rubin, *Better Than Before*

* * *

Questions:

- What is stopping you from being productive?

- Go deeper into each answer. For example, if you said writer's block, then dig to the next level and work out what that block might really be.

- Who do you compare yourself to and why? Is there a way to use that as an inspiration for your next steps?

- How will you overcome these mindset issues to be more productive?

13. Healthy productivity

This is just an overview of how health can impact productivity. For more detail, check out *The Healthy Writer: Reduce your Pain, Improve your Health and Build a Writing Career for the Long Term*, by Joanna Penn and Dr. Euan Lawson.

> Disclaimer: I am not a medical doctor and this chapter is based on my opinion and experience. I'm also not going to be talking in detail about mental health. Please seek medical advice from your doctor if you have health issues.

* * *

You are not just a brain

You are a writer, so you probably spend a lot of time inside your brain thinking creative and interesting thoughts, or learning new things, or getting lost inside a story. But your brain lives inside a physical body and if that body is not well, then your brain can't function properly.

If you want to be more productive, you need to address your physical and mental health as well as your working practices.

"To keep the body in good health is a duty, otherwise we shall not be able to keep our mind strong and clear."

Buddha

Your health is like an onion. There are many layers to work through.

As you peel away the layers, you'll inevitably find more beneath. You can't rush the process, as the physical body can't get fit in one day, or drop that excess weight overnight (as much as we might wish it would!). Here are some of my layers.

Back in my old consulting day job, I lived with almost constant headaches and bi-monthly migraines. I popped painkillers several times a day alongside lattes and banana bread to keep myself going with sugar and caffeine, which also made me gain weight. When I left the open-plan office to work from home as a writer, I discovered the problem was the environment. As an introvert, I couldn't cope with the amount of stimulation and once I was able to work in the quiet, my head pain mostly went away. I rarely get migraines now, perhaps two in the last eight years instead of two per month. So I dealt with that layer through environmental change, but removing constant painkillers revealed the next level.

Once I was working from home, I ended up with Repetitive Strain Injury in my right arm as well as lower back pain, both common in the writing community. I had a home ergonomic review and moved to working at a stand/sit desk. When I sit, I use a Swiss ball, not a chair, so I have constant micro-movement in my back and can also stretch over it. When I write in cafés, I use a Nexstand riser for my laptop and external keyboard, plus I dictate more and record my podcasts standing up. Yoga several times a week helps a great deal for functional movement and eases any residual back pain, and I don't have a car so I walk every day as well as doing longer walks at the weekend. I've recently started weight training for the weaker muscles in my back and shoulders to correct my writer's postural slump which had started pressing on nerves in my arms. Like most writers in their mid-40s, I also have to be careful with my diet.

As you can see, I'm a work in progress as much as anyone else! But what about you?

Do a body scan right now. Think about each area of your body.

What hurts? How's your posture? What are you unhappy with physically? What health issues might be affecting your productivity? What's the first layer of your onion? What could you do about that in the next 24 hours?

Your layers will be different to my layers and some of the underlying issues might go all the way back to things you learned as a child. But believe me, this is worth working on. Your body is yours from cradle to grave, and if you want to keep your brain happy, you need to look after the body it lives in.

Sustainable productivity versus spike productivity

"Beyond a certain point, doing more or working harder is actually counterproductive. Your energy and concentration levels dip, your frustration level increases and if you're not careful, you could be on the slippery slope to creative burnout."

Mark McGuinness, *Productivity for Creative People*

There will be times when you have deadlines for your writing as well as for the rest of your life, so you will need to push harder. Planning your time becomes more important so you don't burn out. If you push yourself too fast, too hard, for too long, you will not be able to sustain your creativity for the long term, and writing is a lifelong career for those who want it to be.

Burn-out is rife in the indie author community, where the rapid release model of writing fast and publishing quickly has been taken to extremes. This can definitely work for some people, but you need to look after your physical and mental health in order to continue to work at your best.

Schedule time for rest, relaxation and play

"Regularly resting your brain improves the quality of your deep work. When you work, work hard. When you're done, be done."

Cal Newport, *Deep Work*

Be gentle with yourself. Life is for living, not just for writing. Build a buffer into your schedule. Make sure that if things happen unexpectedly, you still have time to manage everything instead of going completely nuts.

Rest and relaxation are part of creativity. You're not being lazy, you're filling the creative well. I read a lot, go for long walks and enjoy traveling, art galleries, museums and bookshops. What is rest, relaxation and play for you?

Sort out your sleep

"Sleep is the single most effective thing we can do to reset our brain and body health every day."

Matthew Walker, *Why We Sleep*

Sleep is one of my top priorities and I get eight hours most nights. I have a very dark bedroom, no screens except my Kindle on night mode for reading, and I wear earplugs and an eye mask. I usually wake without an alarm. When I do have difficult times or when I'm feeling miserable, the best thing for me to do is sleep. I will send myself to bed in the afternoon if it feels like everything is falling apart.

I know how lucky I am to be able to sleep this way, and if you have young children, then, of course, things will be difficult for a while. But there are many other causes of sleep issues and you can work through those. For example, if you get back pain, when was the last time you bought a new mattress or pillow? Do you have the right kind for your body shape? Is your room cool enough? Do you have screens in the bedroom? Is it dark enough? If your partner snores, do you wear earplugs or could you move to another room sometimes? (I have a camping mattress in my study for when snoring becomes too much of an issue but usually earplugs are enough!)

Writing is tough on your brain. It's a mental workout, so you need sleep for recovery. If you can sort out your sleep, everything else may become much easier, so take the time to consider how that might be possible.

If you're struggling with sleep or you really want to understand why sleep is so important, read *Why We Sleep* by Matthew Walker. It's an excellent book about something we take for granted and yet can have a profound impact on our health and productivity.

Consider your natural rhythms and cycles

We all have different rhythms and cycles in a day and a month, in a year and across the seasons. It will depend on where you live and the light levels at different times of the year, your hormones and your body type, as well as where you are in your life, so of course, it will be different for everyone and also change across your lifespan.

There are also cycles within the creative process of writing a book. When I finish a novel, I've given everything and I'm exhausted. I need a break and usually a few months off to do other things. I am not one of those authors who writes a book every 45 days, which is why I have other parts to my creative business. You need to consider when you work best and schedule your creative time to fit this.

When do you have the most creative energy?

I'm a morning person so I do my writing in the morning and then I do publishing, marketing, and business tasks in the afternoon. In the evenings, I read or watch TV with my husband, or go for a walk or socialize. I live in the UK, and toward the end of the year, mid-November and December, I start to slow down and need more rest. It's also party season, so I want to be more sociable and tend to catch up with people I haven't seen in a long time. So, I'm not that productive work-wise in December and I'm fine with that. But something in my creative cycle loves January and the beginning of the new year, which is when I kick things up a notch and get writing again.

You can't be productive every day, every month, every year

It just doesn't work like that. You are not the Terminator. You cannot just go, go, go and never stop. Trust me, I've tried!

Think about your creative cycles for a day, a month and for the year, as well as where you are in the cycle of your life. What can you do to be more productive while respecting those cycles?

Get moving!

Your body loves to move. Really, it does! You're designed to move a lot, but of course, as writers, or sedentary desk workers, we often end up turning movement into dreaded exercise, and behave in ways that prevent our bodies from moving well.

I try not to use the word 'exercise' anymore because it feels like punishment or calorie offset. I think about **movement that makes me feel good.** Yoga makes me feel good and I feel strong and invigorated after spinning or weight training. Walking in nature makes me happy and longer walks are satisfying in so many ways. I've started doing salsa and that makes me laugh as I am so bad at it, but it's certainly fun!

By framing these things as movement rather than exercise, my attitude has shifted. I *want* to move because it makes me feel good, and that positive reinforcement makes me want to keep doing it.

What's your attitude to movement right now? How could movement help you to become more productive?

Eat well

The writing profession can be really unhealthy. It's sedentary for most people and inevitably, snacking at your desk can result in excess weight and bad posture that translates to eye strain, back, neck and shoulder pain and a host of other problems.

This is not a diet book and it is a huge subject with so many variables, so I'm not going to go into details here. However, I will challenge you as I challenge myself: Are you making the most of your wonderful physical body? Are you treating yourself well by eating food that will help you to become more productive, happier and healthier?

If not, why not? What changes are you willing to make in your eating behavior? What can you do in the next 24 hours that will start you in the right direction?

Depression, anxiety and chronic pain

Many writers suffer from mental health issues, with some of the most common being depression, anxiety and chronic pain. Some people even become writers because it's one of the few professions that can be managed alongside cycles of pain or mood variation.

It's particularly important to consider mental health in the area of productivity because some of my suggestions won't be right for you. For example, you may want to get a first draft done and might have scheduled daily writing sessions, but then you enter a particular phase of your health and you can't write. That's OK. Don't feel guilty about it.

Instead, think about your creativity and writing as periodic and write when you can. There are no rules.

We all have periods of mental health challenge and there's more that could help in *The Healthy Writer.*

For depression, in particular, listen to this interview with award-winning author, Michaelbrent Collings, where he shares how he manages his writing and family life alongside periods of severe depression:

TheCreativePenn.com/depression

Become part of a community

Loneliness can affect your physical and mental health and it is surprisingly common among authors. I discovered this when I left my day job and started working from home back in 2011. I'm an introvert, so I enjoy being alone and silent, but it can also be really isolating without other people around. Some days, it's easy to feel like you're alone in a bubble where other people don't even exist.

Once I realized this wasn't a healthy way to live, I started working in the London Library and now I write in a café, albeit with noise-canceling headphones, and occasionally in a co-working space. Just being around other people makes you aware that you're not alone in the world, so at least get out of the house every day if you work from home.

Writing a book is also a journey that most will not understand. Your family and friends love you, but they are not the best support for this area of your life, so you need to find a community, whether that's online or off, or a combination of both.

I know this is hard, and when I started writing, I couldn't imagine meeting others like me, but over time, it will happen — if you make the effort. I met many of my writer friends on Twitter first and then moved to having coffee later. I call it 'friend dating,' and like real dating, you might have to try a few before a friendship sticks. I'm also a member of the Alliance of Independent Authors and meet up with other people at conferences like the London Book Fair and also chat on Facebook. You may have to force yourself into some social situations, but eventually, it will be well worth it.

Digital fasting

Becoming a successful author is a process. There are always more things to learn, new technologies to apply and people to meet, compounded by comparisonitis from social media, news overload and overwhelm. Too much input can drive us crazy!

I'm talking to myself here, because I am seriously attached to my iPhone. I use it for listening to audiobooks and podcasts, reading on the Kindle app as well as news apps, searching and learning, taking photos, and yes, also for Instagram and Twitter. But we all need time off technology. One day a week is a good start, and longer periods can be even more rewarding.

Every Sunday, I do a longer walk with my husband, and although my phone is with me for tracking my steps and as a camera, it's on airplane mode. We also have walking and cycling holidays where I am mostly off-grid. The Internet is incredibly valuable, but we all need time away to recharge.

* * *

This chapter covers a lot of ground and of course, you can't fix these things overnight. We all have issues we need to work on. Physical and mental health is a lifelong journey, so enjoy the steps along the way instead of just wishing it were all different. What can you do to start today?

"A journey of a thousand miles begins with a single step."

Chinese proverb

* * *

Questions:

- Why are physical and mental health important for productivity?

- Think of your health like an onion. What is the first layer you need to tackle? What's bothering you right now?

- Where is your resistance around health issues?

- How are you going to ensure self-care in order to be productive for the long term?

Conclusion and next steps

There are a lot of tips and tools in this book and I hope that you have discovered some new ideas that will help you to become more productive. But I don't want to leave you overwhelmed, so here are my top three tips, the things that should provide you with the most leverage for your next steps. If you do nothing else, do these.

(1) Choose your focus and eliminate everything else

So much of what we do isn't necessary in order to achieve our goals. If you can pare back all those extra activities, even for a short time, you will have the time and headspace to beat overwhelm and achieve your writing goals.

(2) Schedule your creative time and don't miss it

If you want to write your first book, produce more books, or make more money with your writing, then you must do this. No excuses. Start using a schedule and make your creative time sacred.

(3) Sort out your sleep

Physical health is critical to productivity as well as happiness, and sleep is the best way to recover from a busy day, recharge for tomorrow and give your creative mind time to figure out interesting things for you to write next.

* * *

Now it's time for you to put this book into action and become more productive while I get back to writing the next book!

Need more help on your author journey?

Sign up for my *free* Author 2.0 Blueprint and email series, and receive useful information on writing, publishing, book marketing, and making a living with your writing:

www.TheCreativePenn.com/blueprint

* * *

Love podcasts? Join me every Monday for
The Creative Penn Podcast where I talk about writing, publishing, book marketing and the author business.
Available on your favorite podcast app.

Find the backlist episodes at:

www.TheCreativePenn.com/podcast

Appendix 1: Bibliography

You can find a downloadable version of this at:

TheCreativePenn.com/productivitydownload

Atomic Habits: An Easy and Proven Way to Build Good Habits and Break Bad Ones — James Clear

Better Than Before: What I Learned About Making and Breaking Habits — To Sleep More, Quit Sugar, Procrastinate Less and Generally Build a Happier Life — Gretchen Rubin

Co-writing a Book: Collaboration and Co-creation for Writers — Joanna Penn and J. Thorn

Daily Rituals: How Artists Work — Mason Currey

Deep Work: Rules for Focused Success in a Distracted World — Cal Newport

Dictate Your Book: How to Write your Book Faster, Better and Smarter — Monica Leonelle

Don't Read this Book: Time Management for Creative People — Donald Roos

Essentialism: The Disciplined Pursuit of Less — Greg McKeown

Foolproof Dictation: A Non-Nonsense System for Effective and Rewarding Dictation — Christopher Downing

How to Make a Living with your Writing — Joanna Penn

How to Write Non-Fiction: Turn Your Knowledge into Words — Joanna Penn

Manage Your Day-To-Day edited — Jocelyn K. Glei (editor)

On Being a Dictator: Using Dictation to be a Better Writer — Kevin J. Anderson

On Writing: A Memoir of the Craft — Stephen King

Productivity for Creative People: How to Get Creative Work Done in an Always On World — Mark McGuinness

Seth Godin blog post on busyness - https://seths.blog/2018/07/busyness/

Steal Like An Artist: 10 Things Nobody Told You About Being Creative — Austin Kleon

The Artist's Way — Julia Cameron

The Big Leap — Gay Hendricks

The Compound Effect: Jumpstart Your Income, Your Life, Your Success — Darren Hardy

The Healthy Writer: Reduce your Pain, Improve your Health, and Build a Writing Career for the Long Term — Joanna Penn and Dr. Euan Lawson

The ONE Thing: The Surprisingly Simple Truth Behind Extraordinary Results — Gary Keller and Jay Papasan

The War of Art: Break Through the Blocks and Win Your Inner Creative Battles — Steven Pressfield

The Writers Guide to Training your Dragon: Mastering Speech Recognition Software to Dictate your Book and Supercharge your Writing Workflow — Scott Baker

Turning Pro: Tap Your Inner Power and Create Your Life's Work — Steven Pressfield

Virtual Freedom: How to Work with Virtual Staff to Buy More Time, Become More Productive, and Build Your Dream Business — Chris Ducker

Why We Sleep: Unlocking the Power of Sleep and Dreams — Matthew Walker

* * *

You can find all my books for authors at:

www.TheCreativePenn.com/books

Most of them are available in audiobook format, as well as ebook and paperback.

Appendix 2: Question List

You can find a downloadable version of this at:

TheCreativePenn.com/productivitydownload

"Productivity is the amount of useful output created for every hour of work we do. Did I spend my day producing enough benefit for all the time invested?"

Seth Godin, Business/busyness

* * *

Chapter 1: What is stopping you from being more productive?

- What is your why? What is driving you toward your goal? What will keep you going when things get tough?

- What is stopping you from being productive right now? What do you need to address in order to move forward?

- What is your specific goal and the date by which you want to achieve it? [Write it down!]

- What can you put in place to stay accountable?

Chapter 2: Goal setting

- What goals do you currently have in your life? What is your primary goal?

- What stage of the author journey are you at? What is the best goal for your current stage? What could wait until later?

Chapter 3: Deadlines

- What is the deadline for your goal? Have you written it somewhere you can see it regularly?

- What can you do to make yourself more accountable?

Chapter 4: Busy work vs. important work

- Write down everything you have to do, or review your list. How much of it is 'busy work'? How much can wait until a later stage of the process?

- How are you balancing busy work with important work and urgent work? What things fall into these categories for you?

Chapter 5: Saying no and setting boundaries

- What are you struggling to say no to? Where do you need to set boundaries to protect your creative time?

- Write your own Not To Do list

- How could you set boundaries in order to protect your time for what you really want to achieve?

- How much are you giving into distraction? Have you turned off notifications on your phone and computer?

- What could you do if you are still struggling?

Chapter 6: How to find the time to write

- Are you scheduling your writing time at the moment? If not, why not? Where is your resistance?

- Do you have an accurate view of how you spend your time? If not, track a week of activities including TV and gaming.

- What are you going to give up in order to find time for your writing?

- Have you done the calculation on how much time you need for that first draft? Or revision time or whatever you need.

- Have you scheduled your next block of writing time?

Chapter 7: Make the most of your writing time

- What does your creative setup and ritual look like?

- How will you stop distractions and interruptions?

- Have you tried timed writing? If not, why not?

- How will you measure your progress?

- How could you write faster?

- Are there any other ways that will help you make the most of your time writing?

Chapter 8: Dictation

- Why might you consider dictation? How might it help your writing?

- What's stopping you from dictating? How can you work through those issues in order to try it?

- What method of dictation might work for you?

- What tools do you need to get started?

Chapter 9: Co-writing and collaboration

- Why do you want to co-write or collaborate with another writer? What are the pros and cons for you?

- Why are you a good fit as a partnership?

- Have you laid out working process, deadlines, money etc in a written document?

- How will you make sure that your collaboration works for the long-term?

Chapter 10: Outsourcing

- Do you currently work with different freelancers? How much do you do yourself? How much do you WANT to do yourself?

- What are your zones of incompetence, competence, excellence and genius? Are you spending too much time in the wrong zone?

- What is stopping you from hiring more help right now? How can you remedy that so you have more time to create?

- Make a list of everything you do, and split it into logical groupings

- Eliminate tasks that really don't need doing – or don't need doing right now

- Could any of the tasks be automated?

- Where can you look for freelancers / virtual assistants?

- How will you work effectively with the freelancers / virtual assistants?

Chapter 11: Productivity tools

- Is there a part of your process that could be improved with a tool?

- Which tool/s could help you to become more productive?

Chapter 12: The productive writer mindset

- What is stopping you from being productive?

- Go deeper into each answer. For example, if you said writer's block, then dig to the next level and work out what that block might really be.

- Who do you compare yourself to and why? Is there a way to use that as inspiration for your next steps?

- How will you overcome these mindset issues to be more productive?

Chapter 13: Healthy productivity

- Why are physical and mental health important for productivity?

- Think of your health like an onion. What is the first layer you need to tackle? What's bothering you right now?

- Where is your resistance around health issues?

- How are you going to ensure self-care in order to be productive for the long term?

Conclusion and next steps

- What three things can you do to improve your productivity in the next 7 days?

Appendix 3:
Tools and Resources

The following resources are mentioned in the book, listed below for reference. You can find a downloadable version of this at: TheCreativePenn.com/productivitydownload

Chapter 3: Deadlines

Twitter hashtags #5amwritersclub #writingcommunity

National Novel Writing Month www.NaNoWriMo.org

My journey from idea to first novel www.TheCreativePenn.com/firstnovel

Chapter 5: Saying no and setting boundaries

Freedom app to block internet access: www.freedom.to

Chapter 7: Make the most of your writing time

Google Calendar: calendar.google.com

Nexstand riser for laptop ergonomic positioning on the move: www.TheCreativePenn.com/nexstand

Noise-canceling headphones. I use BOSE Quiet Comfort. www.TheCreativePenn.com/silence

Rain and thunderstorm sounds: www.RainyMood.com

Undercover Soundtrack blog by Roz Morris - mymemoriesofafuturelife.com/category/ undercover-soundtrack

Pomodoro Technique, developed by Francesco Cirillo. - francescocirillo.com/pages/pomodoro-technique

Scrivener writing software - www.TheCreativePenn.com/scrivenersoftware

Chapter 8: Dictation

Nuance Dragon dictation and voice control software: www.nuance.com/en-gb/dragon.html

Dragon Anywhere mobile app: www.nuance.com/ en-gb/dragon/dragon-anywhere.html

For using dictation on your computer:

- Open Google Docs on Chrome Browser. Click Tools -> Voice Typing

- On the Mac, use Edit -> Start Dictation

- On the PC, hold down the Windows key and press H to trigger the dictation toolbar. (This may vary with whatever version of Windows you're on.)

Transcription options:

- Speechpad.com

- Rev.com

- Descript.com

- otter.ai

- Trint.com

Voice recorder I use: Sony ICD-PX333 MP3 recorder: TheCreativePenn.com/sony

Blue Yeti microphone, which I also use for my podcast and recording my online courses: TheCreativePenn.com/blueyeti

Podcast interviews and transcription on dictation: TheCreativePenn.com/dictation

Chapter 9: Co-writing and collaboration

Software for co-writing:

- Google Docs - docs.google.com

- Dropbox - dropbox.com

- Storyshop.io

Discussion with my Mum on co-writing as Penny Appleton and why we decided to stop: TheCreativePenn.com/penny

Payment splitting for co-writers:

- PublishDrive Abacus - publishdrive.com/abacus

- Bundle Rabbit Collaboration - bundlerabbit.com/home/collaborate

For more details, including example contracts, check out *Co-Writing A Book: Collaboration and Co-creation for Writers* by Joanna Penn and J. Thorn.

Chapter 10: Outsourcing

WordPress hosting service with management of plugin updates: TheCreativePenn.com/wpengine

Managed inbox service: InboxDone.com

Vellum for formatting ebook and print books (Mac only): TheCreativePenn.com/vellum

Tutorial on using Vellum for formatting: TheCreativePenn.com/vellum-tutorial

Vetted freelancers who specialise in working with authors: TheCreativePenn.com/reedsy

Freelancer network: Upwork.com

Recommended freelance editors: TheCreativePenn.com/editors

Recommended freelance book cover designers: TheCreativePenn.com/bookcoverdesign

Recommended freelance book formatters: TheCreativePenn.com/formatting

Skype: Skype.com

PayPal: PayPal.com

Password sharing with freelancers: LastPass.com

Yaro Starak's Blog Profits Blueprint:
TheCreativePenn.com/blogblueprint

Chapter 11: Productivity Tools

Backup your work! I use Dropbox.com

Scrivener
- TheCreativePenn.com/scrivenersoftware

Amazon S3 cloud hosting - aws.amazon.com

Google Drive - google.com/drive

Google Calendar: calendar.google.com

Scheduling time across calendars and time zones:
calendly.com

To Do list: Things app (Mac Only)
culturedcode.com/things

Password protection: 1Password.com

Social media scheduling:

- BufferApp.com

- Missinglettr.com

- IFTTT.com

- Zapier.com

- Later.com

Email list forms, hosting and management: Convert Kit: TheCreativePenn.com/convert

Tutorial on how to set up your email list with ConvertKit: TheCreativePenn.com/setup-email-list

Create and host online courses with Teachable: TheCreativePenn.com/teachable

Accounting software:

- Xero.com

- Quickbooks.com

- Freshbooks.com

Freedom app - freedom.to

Chapter 13: Healthy Productivity

Swiss ball I use instead of a chair

Nexstand riser for laptop: TheCreativePenn.com/nexstand

For depression, in particular, listen to this interview with award-winning author, Michaelbrent Collings, where he shares how he manages his writing and family life alongside periods of severe depression: TheCreativePenn.com/depression

Alliance of Independent Authors: TheCreativePenn.com/alliance

About Joanna Penn

Joanna Penn, writing as J.F.Penn, is an Award-nominated, New York Times and USA Today bestselling author of thrillers and dark fantasy, as well as writing inspirational non-fiction for authors.

She is an international professional speaker, podcaster, and award-winning entrepreneur. She lives in Bath, England with her husband and enjoys a nice G&T.

Joanna's award-winning site for writers www.TheCreative-Penn.com helps people to write, publish and market their books through articles, audio, video and online products as well as live workshops.

Love thrillers? www.JFPenn.com

Love travel? www.BooksAndTravel.page

Connect with Joanna
www.TheCreativePenn.com
joanna@TheCreativePenn.com

www.twitter.com/thecreativepenn
www.facebook.com/TheCreativePenn
www.Instagram.com/jfpennauthor
www.youtube.com/thecreativepenn

More Books And Courses From Joanna Penn

Non-Fiction Books for Authors

How to Write Non-Fiction

How to Market a Book

How to Make a Living with your Writing

Productivity for Authors

Business for Authors

The Healthy Writer

Successful Self-Publishing

Co-writing a Book

Public Speaking for Authors,
Creatives and Other Introverts

Career Change

www.TheCreativePenn.com/books

Courses for authors

How to Write a Novel: From Idea to First Draft to Finished Manuscript

How to Write Non-Fiction:
Turn your Knowledge into Words

Productivity for Authors

Content Marketing for Fiction Authors

www.TheCreativePenn.com/courses

Thriller novels as J.F.Penn

The ARKANE supernatural thriller series:

Stone of Fire #1
Crypt of Bone #2
Ark of Blood #3
One Day In Budapest #4
Day of the Vikings #5
Gates of Hell #6
One Day in New York #7
Destroyer of Worlds #8
End of Days #9
Valley of Dry Bones #10

If you like **crime thrillers with an edge of the supernatural**, join Detective Jamie Brooke and museum researcher Blake Daniel, in the London Crime Thriller trilogy:

Desecration #1
Delirium #2
Deviance #3

The Mapwalker dark fantasy series

Map of Shadows #1
Map of Plagues #2

Risen Gods

American Demon Hunters: Sacrifice

A Thousand Fiendish Angels:
Short stories based on Dante's Inferno

The Dark Queen:
An Underwater Archaeology Short Story

More books coming soon.

You can sign up to be notified of new releases, giveaways
and pre-release specials - plus, get a free book!

www.JFPenn.com/free

Printed in Great Britain
by Amazon

59977085R00075